THE EXPERTS APPLAUD SAFE

PRAISE FOR THE AUTHORS OF SAFE FOOD

"With admirable relentlessness, the Center for Science in the Public Interest continues its efforts to improve our eating habits."
—*New York Daily News*

"...the nation's most respected nutrition advocacy group based on science."
—*Boston Globe*

"Largely thanks to the Center's indefatigable pursuit of errant food manufacturers and the FDA, there are now fewer additives in processed foods and drinks."

—*St. Petersburg Times*

"...this group has been unique in bringing to consumer advocacy good health perspectives and priorities..."
—*Medical Tribune*

"Michael Jacobson may just be the most influential man in the food industry. Or, more correctly, outside the food industry—and outside the government."
—*Philadelphia Inquirer*

"Luckily for the rest of us, the Center for Science is performing a vital service as watchdog of our food supply."
—Richard Sax, cookbook author and
Bon Appétit's "Cooking Healthy" co-columnist

EATING WISELY
IN A RISKY WORLD

Michael F. Jacobson, Ph.D.
Lisa Y. Lefferts
Anne Witte Garland

Center for Science in the Public Interest

LIVING PLANET
P R E S S

Los Angeles

Interior design and page layout: Garland Graphics

Interior illustrations: Carole Etow

Printing and binding: The Banta Company

Discounts for bulk orders are available from the publisher. Call (213) 396-0188.

 **Printed on recycled Butte des Morts paper**

ISBN 1-879326-01-9

Manufactured in the United States of America

Library of Congress catalog card number 91-060335

10 9 8 7 6 5 4 3 2 1

We dedicate this book to the people who have the power to ensure a safer food supply: FDA Commissioner David Kessler; USDA Secretary Edward Madigan; U.S. Representatives John Dingell, Kika de la Garza, Henry Waxman, and Ted Weiss; and Senators Robert Dole, Orrin Hatch, Edward Kennedy, Patrick Leahy, and Howard Metzenbaum. With their prompt action, countless numbers of Americans will live longer, healthier lives.

CONTENTS

AUTHORS' ACKNOWLEDGMENTS

We would like to thank numerous colleagues for helping to ensure the accuracy of this book. In particular, we thank the following staff members of the Center for Science in the Public Interest (CSPI): Roger Blobaum and Beth Zimmerman for their guidance and suggestions concerning organic foods, citizen action, and numerous other sections; Victoria Leonard for suggestions on children's nutrition; Bonnie Liebman and Jayne Hurley for reviewing and contributing valuable information to the nutrition sections; Bruce Silverglade for reviewing the food-labeling section; Stephen Schmidt for suggestions on Chapters 1 and 4; Patricia Taylor for writing much of the section on alcoholic beverages; and stalwart intern Vanessa Thompson for preparing the list of mail-order sources of organic food and for help in researching.

Thanks also to CSPI's Ann Backhaus, Svetlana Bekman, Dennis Coyne, Mary Davis, Nicole Farkas, Lorraine Jones, Matthew Merced, and Patrice O'Toole, and to Blair Pillsbury in New York, for their help in research and fact-checking. In addition, thanks to Brad Walrod, who produced chart layouts, helped prepare the manuscript for design, and cheerfully shared his expert knowledge of the QuarkXPress page-layout program.

We made liberal use of many useful, free U.S. Department of Agriculture publications on safe food-handling methods.

We are grateful to the following colleagues for their thoughtful comments on portions of the manuscript: Karim Ahmed, Judy Bellin, Tom Devine, Carol Tucker Foreman, Jay Goldring, Edward Groth III, Sandra Marquardt, Lawrie Mott and other Natural Resources Defense Council staff, and Mitch Zeller.

We especially thank Dinah Berland of Living Planet Press for her many editorial suggestions and decisions, and Stephen Tukel and Joshua Horwitz of Living Planet, for recognizing the need for a book that provides comprehensive, factual advice for consumers on food safety.

Finally, we would like to acknowledge with gratitude the personal support of David and Kenneth Garland, Mark Heinicke, Eugene Lefferts, Donna and Howard Lenhoff, Marcia Rosen, and Iris Wilbur.

FOREWORD

We need safer food. Headline after depressing headline has hammered home the seriousness of the problems. Across the country, water supplies have been contaminated with pesticides. In New England, salmonellosis from eggs is considered an epidemic. In the Midwest, more than 16,000 consumers in Illinois fell ill, and more than a dozen died, due to salmonellosis from contaminated milk sold by a major supermarket chain. On the West Coast, 29 people died from listeriosis after they ate Mexican-style cheese, and hundreds were stricken after they ate watermelons contaminated with the pesticide aldicarb.

The litany of horrors continues with illnesses from bacteria-ridden chicken, deadly vibrio infections from raw shellfish, and gastroenteritis outbreaks on Caribbean cruise ships, at summer camps, and in nursing homes. In addition, Americans have suffered through crises related to Alar in apples, antibiotics in milk, and potentially deadly sulfite preservatives in salads.

Though government officials assert that pesticide regulations ensure safety, most of those regulations fail to protect children, who consume more food relative to their weight than adults and whose immune and nervous systems have not fully formed.

Moreover, pesticides cause cancer in farmers and farm workers. And millions of pounds of fertilizer and pesticides are polluting our air, land, and water. It's no wonder that industry's own surveys consistently find that three out of four shoppers consider residues such as pesticides to be a serious health hazard.

The contamination of our food supply, fortunately, is not an altogether grim and hopeless story. Each and every one of us—whether a consumer, a farmer, a grocer, or an employee of a giant food manufacturing company—can help move America toward a safer, more healthful food supply. *Safe Food* tells us how.

For instance, organic and sustainable farming practices, which get farmers off the chemical treadmill caused by increased pesticide resistance of insects and weeds, benefit farmers, consumers, and the environment. More consumers are responding to the advantages of organically grown food and are generally buying more fresh fruits and vegetables instead of canned counterparts. It is like a good genie coming out of the bottle. A critical momentum of buyer knowledge and action is now influencing both the marketplace and the agendas of the local, state, and federal governmental agencies that are supposed to protect our food supply. Increasing that influence is one purpose of this book.

If you ask "What can I do?" *Safe Food* responds: "Plenty." Immediately, *Safe Food* gives you the information you need to buy safer and more nutritious food with less fat, salt, sugar, and pesticide residues. And it tells you, simply and directly, how to prepare that food to avoid bacterial infections. For more than a few people, growing some of your own food and preparing more of your meals, instead of relying on the more expensive processed "convenience" stuff, can make sense right away.

Safe Food also tells you what you can do as a citizen to make the government regulators reflect not industry's demands, but your demands to clean up the food supply. *Safe Food* can open up practical possibilities in your kitchen, in your grocery market, and on farms to promote the integrity of the nation's food.

All it takes is a "can-do" attitude and an enthusiasm for working with other citizens in a common quest for safer food. Just reading *Safe Food* and becoming part of the national safe-food movement—spearheaded by the Center of Science in the Public Interest and other groups—will sharpen your food-buying and civic skills. And being involved will give you a wonderful feeling of satisfaction that you, a single individual in a populous nation, can actually make an important difference for a better world.

—Ralph Nader
Washington, D.C.
April 1991

INTRODUCTION

TAKING A NEW LOOK AT YOUR FOOD

If you've been confused by conflicting newspaper headlines that one day scream that "everything in our food causes cancer" and the next reassure you that "America has the world's safest food supply," this book is for you.

The Center for Science in the Public Interest (CSPI) has sought for 20 years to improve the safety of America's food supply and has generated headlines about dangers of antibiotics in milk, sodium nitrite in bacon, caffeine in coffee and soft drinks, and urethane in brandy. Yet despite all the expert information we have on a given issue or substance, even we are sometimes unsure whether something is safe or not.

In the early days of this century, Upton Sinclair's book, *The Jungle*, documented the horrible conditions under which meat was processed. Sinclair's focus was on rats, flies, feces, and other visible causes of illness. But, with every passing year, agriculture and food manufacturing became ever more complex. Scientific researchers developed ever more sensitive detection methods, and concerns about food safety moved to the microscopic and molecular levels.

The enforcement files of the Food and Drug Administration and local health departments prove that flies and rodents remain problems in all too many factories and restaurants. But invisible organisms and chemicals have brought new problems and raised new concerns. Recent research tells us that: pathogenic bacteria can grow in milk at temperatures once thought safe; use of pesticides and veterinary drugs by farmers and processors leaves minuscule amounts of cancer-promoting substances

in foods; industrial pollutants, such as PCBs and dioxins—chemicals that have no business being in our food—
get in anyhow; packaging contaminants and food
additives increase slightly the risks of cancer, birth defects,
or behavioral changes; and some dangerous substances
have been in our food supply for hundreds or thousands
of years.

Indeed, protecting our food supply has become a lot
more complicated, especially with the advent of "factory"
farming, plastic containers, microwave ovens, and frozen
meals. New technologies leave unexpected substances in
our food, and it is the job of scientists to determine
whether those substances are safe or dangerous. In all too
many cases, scientists can't come up with definitive
answers. In many cases, the risks are clearly minor. In
those cases, government officials must decide if the risks
are truly negligible and simply not worth further attention—or serious enough to pose a risk to a significant
number of people in a nation of 250 million.

Sometimes it seems as if the newer and more invisible the risk, the more emotional the battle about its safety.
We've seen highly charged controversies in recent years
over pesticides, milk-stimulating hormones, and food irradiation. Each of those agents was both new to the food
supply and posed a real or perceived possibility of risk.
Moreover, many people are skeptical of any new technology. While some of the opposition to innovation may
appear to be irrational paranoia, it's worth remembering
some of industry's mistakes. Americans have been treated
to a wide range of "technological miracles," ranging from
radiation-emitting fluoroscopes in shoe stores to drugs
such as thalidomide. These and other innovations that
later proved disastrous should be enough to teach us the
importance of moving slowly and cautiously before sub-
jecting an entire nation to a technology or chemical that
appears, at first, to be worthwhile.

Intensifying public concern is the fact that some food risks, although minuscule, are not under a person's control. Thus, even people who smoke cigarettes, enjoy sky-diving, or drive without their seatbelts might object to lesser but involuntary risks foisted upon them by the food industry. The common retort that chemical X is a zillion times safer than flying into O'Hare Airport just doesn't wash.

Moreover, some new technologies raise hackles because they introduce broader problems. In the case of BGH/BST, the larger concern is biotechnology and genetic engineering. In the case of pesticides, it is harm to wildlife, the environment, and farm workers. For irradiation, the concerns are environmental pollution from and worker exposure to radioactive materials. In all these cases, the challenge is to weigh all the risks and benefits to society (including nonhealth problems), and to maximize any benefits while minimizing or eliminating the risks.

Many recent food-safety controversies are reminiscent of the early attacks on microwave ovens. The real problem caused by radiation leakage from the ovens led many people to oppose them. However, when industry figured out how to prevent the leakage and eliminate virtually all significant risk, consumers were reassured, and microwave ovens became commonplace and accepted kitchen tools.

In *Safe Food*, we have sought to evaluate the risks and make informed judgments about the safety of dozens of organisms and foreign materials in food. Some judgments are easy. Everyone agrees that eating raw shellfish is like playing Russian roulette. But oftentimes the risk is tiny or uncertain. In such cases, individuals can either ignore the risk or avoid it by making different buying decisions and, thereby, simultaneously encouraging industry to solve the problem for everyone.

However, a risk that is trivial for a given individual

may pose a large enough risk to an entire population to warrant government action. In fact, this book was written with the assumption that an important mission and responsibility of government food-safety agencies is to protect consumers from minor risks over which they have little control, as well as from the major ones that should be acted upon at once. That's what government agencies such as the Food and Drug Administration and the U. S. Department of Agriculture were established, in part, to do.

Meanwhile, you can learn how to eat wisely in this risky world. We've designed this book to help you make some vital choices—to inform you about the food issues we all face, help you decide which ones might be of most immediate concern to you and your family, and provide you with ideas about what you can do right now. Think of *Safe Food* as your navigator through the complex maze of risks to our food supply. It will point you in the direction of safer food choices at home and in the marketplace, and ways to make your food supply safer for yourself and your family in the future. Here's how to use it.

HOW TO USE THIS BOOK

Safe Food is designed to be easy to read as well as to pick up any time as a handy reference. First of all, we suggest that you read Chapter 1, "Safe Food Choices," to get an overview of the kinds of food problems that currently exist and what to do about them. This chapter also contains a summary of the five most important things you can do to ensure that the food you eat and prepare for your family is the safest possible. It examines your food risks in light of your diet as a whole and debunks some of the most common fallacies about food safety. In Chapter 1, you'll also find dozens of ways to improve your diet from a nutritional standpoint. This chapter also highlights techniques for "Defensive eating"—an important summary of food-safety precautions for pregnant women, nursing mothers, older adults, people who are HIV-positive or have AIDS, and others with weakened immune systems or food allergies who need to be especially careful about what they eat.

Next, in Chapters 2 through 5, you can check out the produce, grains, dairy foods, meat, poultry, eggs, fish and shellfish that you eat every day and what's right or wrong with each one. Within each chapter is an assortment of "Safe Food Choices" you can begin making right now, every time you shop, prepare, and store your food. You'll also learn what actions you might take to improve the food available to you in the future—action that will help to determine how food is grown, how stores market it to us, and how the government regulates food safety.

Chapter 6, "What's Safe to Drink?" examines the safety of drinking water, soft drinks, alcohol, and other beverages, and tells you which are best. Chapter 7, "The Truth about Additives," explains the ins and outs of food additives—which ones are safe and which to avoid.

Chapter 8, "The Safe Food Kitchen," is a handy reference for every cook—whether you're setting up a kitchen for the first time or have been preparing meals for years. Here you'll learn things your mother never taught you—about choosing, storing, and preparing safe food.

If you want to reduce food risks even more, we let you know how to take political action to make your food supply even safer. Chapter 9, "The Safe Food Agenda," provides you with the most important government reforms that are needed right now to improve food safety in the United States.

And finally, turn to Chapter 10, "More Food for Thought and Action," whenever you want to dip into our catalogue of safe-food resources, such as cookbooks, newsletters, helpful organizations, and hotlines. We've also included a state-by-state list of mail-order sources of organic foods, a letter calling for important changes in your supermarket, plus sample letters for writing to your elected representatives and government agencies to press for food-safety reforms.

So, now it's time to look at the food on your dinner plate in a way you've never done before. But before you start reading, you'd better check the label on that bag of cookies and put the milk back in the fridge!

CHAPTER 1
SAFE FOOD CHOICES

SAFE FOOD CHOICES

Eating is one of life's greatest pleasures. Enjoying a delicious, home-cooked meal with friends or family ought to be relaxing and fun. No one wants to sit down to dinner and have to worry about pesticides lurking in the broccoli, salmonella in the chicken, and unpronounceable veterinary drugs in the milk—not to mention the saturated fat in the steak.

Still, while government and industry assure us that "America has the world's safest food supply," many difficult questions persist. What are the long-term results of eating fruits and vegetables that have been sprayed with pesticides? What assurance can government and industry offer that the milk we feed our children is safe? The answers are unimpressive. Report after report from government, public-interest groups, and think tanks—including the National Academy of Sciences—documents problems. Too much of our food supply is contaminated with dangerous, questionable, or inadequately tested pesticides, bacteria, industrial pollutants, packaging contaminants, veterinary drugs, and additives. Even the government acknowledges that food-borne illnesses are increasing—illnesses that cause the deaths of thousands of Americans every year. And that's before basic nutritional risks are considered.

This chapter will give you an overview of your best bets for eating wisely, taking all these factors into account. First, we'll shed light on some of the fallacies that permeate food-safety debates, separating serious problems from spurious claims. Then we'll provide you with five steps to safer food. We'll also pinpoint specific problems with our food supply and what you can do about them, and close the chapter with a guide to nutrition in general.

FOOD SAFETY AND FOOD RISKS: FACTS VS. FALLACIES

More often than not, just when you've been told that some additive or pesticide is hazardous (nitrites in bacon, for instance, or saccharin in soft drinks, or Alar in apples), someone else comes along and claims that there's nothing to worry about. "They fed the rats the equivalent of 50 pounds of bacon—so of course they got cancer," goes the argument. Or, "You'd have to eat a truckload of apples a day to get cancer from the pesticides that are sprayed on them."

Many people ignore the whole debate out of frustration. Others assume that everything they eat will cause cancer. A far more sensible approach is to identify your greatest risks first. Take stock of your overall dietary problems as well as other major hazards to your health—smoking, unsafe working conditions, hazards in and around your home, driving habits—and take the necessary steps to change them. Then you can begin to make informed choices about the safety of your food.

It's important to keep your food risks in proper perspective. With produce, for instance, the riskiest thing you could do would be to stop eating fruits and vegetables altogether. The less risky choice would be to eat plenty of them, pesticides and all. The least risky alternatives would be to buy certified organic produce, and to wash and prepare fruits and vegetables in ways that minimize your exposure to pesticide residues and bacteria.

Here's more help in sorting out some food-risk misconceptions from reality:

Fallacy: *America's food supply is the safest in the world.*

Fact: Maybe it is. But this claim, which is made by the government, industry, and industry-supported front groups and academic consultants, has never been proven. And, with some 9,000 people dying each year from food poisoning alone[1]—not to mention the harder-to-quantify long-term effects of toxins or carcinogens in food—it's clear that America's food supply could and should be safer.

Fallacy: *All food additives are harmful.*

Fact: Of the hundreds of chemicals currently added intentionally to our food, the vast majority are safe. A few are not safe, at least at the levels at which they're being consumed, or aren't safe for certain sensitive individuals. For other additives, there is no conclusive evidence to show whether they're safe. Some additives, such as calcium propionate or ascorbic acid, are positively beneficial. (The additives to avoid, and those which are safe, are listed in Chapter 7.)

Fallacy: *We don't need to be concerned about a few insignificant carcinogens in our food—especially when cancer rates are going down.*

Fact: Actually, even cancer experts can't agree about whether cancer rates are going down or up.[2] Cancer isn't a single disease, but many different diseases. Depending on what types of cancer are being studied and what is being measured—new cases or deaths—experts can come up with either optimistic or pessimistic conclusions about cancer trends. But the fact remains that some 500,000 Americans die every year from cancer, and that statistic alone argues for better cancer prevention. As an individual, you can protect yourself from the major, well-documented cancer risks, such as smoking and excessive fat in your diet. As for the comparatively minor or harder-to-prove risks, such as pesticides in food, why not protect yourself if you can?

Fallacy: *The carcinogens in our food supply are at safe levels.*

Fact: For most carcinogens, no one knows for sure whether there is a "safe" level.[3] Even a very small amount may increase your risk of cancer slightly. The larger the amount, the larger the risk. So for carcinogens the question isn't, "Are they safe?" but, "Are the risks they pose acceptable?" When it comes to unnecessary chemicals, such as artificial colors, it doesn't make sense to accept any risk whatsoever.

Fallacy: *The risk from natural carcinogens in food is much greater than the cancer risk from additives, pesticides, and contaminants.*

Fact: No one really knows the relative risks of artificial vs. natural carcinogens in food—not even those scientists who have made headlines with this assertion. In fact, many so-called "natural carcinogens" are not considered carcinogenic by the World Health Organization, the

Let them eat falsehoods

The food and chemical industries have many effective ways to tout the safety of their products, including sponsoring massive television and magazine advertising, maintaining powerful trade associations that lobby Congress, financing self-serving scientific studies, hiring "objective" academic spokespersons, and funding so-called "consumer organizations" that are really corporate front groups.

One such organization, the American Council on Science and Health, is funded largely by food, chemical, and other companies. It was particularly visible in 1989 during the uproar over Alar in apples, with its full-page newspaper ads declaring "Our food supply is safe," and its film, "Big Fears, Little Risks."

Next time you see a reasonable-looking ad singing the praises of pesticides or extolling the virtues of, say, beef or sugar, look at who sponsored the ad and take what it says with—ahem—a grain of salt.

National Toxicology Program, and other authorities.[4] Many naturally occurring chemicals need to be better tested (after all, "natural" doesn't mean "safe" any more than "synthetic" means "unsafe"). But the fact that some carcinogens occur naturally certainly doesn't justify adding synthetic carcinogens to the food supply.

Fallacy: *Everything causes cancer if the dose is high enough, so the enormous doses used in animal tests don't prove anything.*

Fact: Most chemicals do not cause cancer, no matter how high the dose. In addition, most of the chemicals studied that do cause cancer at high doses also cause cancer at lower doses.[5] While high-dose animal tests may be questioned on ethical grounds, they are still the most reliable method currently available for determining whether a chemical is likely to cause cancer in humans. If lower, more realistic doses were used, scientists would have to use thousands of times more laboratory animals for each experiment, and nobody wants—or could afford—that.

Fallacy: *One part per million of a chemical is like a drop in a swimming pool, which can't possibly be harmful.*

Fact: Companies invariably defend chemicals by saying that the amount in food is obviously too little to cause a problem. Of course, the less of a dangerous chemical the better. But, in fact, just as one bacterium can sometimes lead to a serious infection, unbelievably small amounts of some chemicals can increase the risk of cancer or miscarriage. We can't assume that a chemical present at levels of one part in a million, or one in a billion, will be harmless.

Fallacy: *The experts know what the risks are.*

Fact: Risk assessment is an inexact science at best. On one hand, we need to rely on the opinions of scientific experts because most of us don't have the time, resources, or expertise to evaluate the latest scientific information ourselves. On the other hand, we shouldn't simply accept what the "experts" say without question, for several reasons:

➤ Risk estimates based on animal-test results may be too high or too low. The drug thalidomide had no effect on laboratory mice or rats, but in humans it caused severe birth defects in babies whose mothers took it for "morning sickness" during pregnancy. Other substances, such as dioxins,[6] are apparently more toxic to some laboratory animals than to people.

➤ No one knows the combined risk of consuming small amounts of many different additives and chemical residues. Risk estimates for a single chemical don't reflect how the chemical may interact with other chemicals to which a person may be exposed. In the laboratory, chemicals are usually tested one at a time. But in the real world, we're exposed to a multitude of substances that may interact together to increase or decrease the effects of that chemical. Ideally, chemicals should be tested individually, as well as in combination with aspirin, caffeine, and other chemicals that people consume every day.

➤ The government claims that it consistently overestimates the risks of pesticides and other chemicals. But a study by John C. Bailar III, Ph.D., a science advisor for the U.S. Office of Disease Prevention and Health Promotion and a professor at McGill University, sheds doubt on that contention. Bailar examined the data for one chemical that had been so thoroughly studied, it could be used to measure the accuracy of government predictions against actual test results on animals. His conclusions were significant: the government methods "substantially" underestimated the effects at low doses (by as much as nine times).[7]

➤ In calculating risks, scientists and government regulators generally fail to consider important ethical questions, such as whether a given risk is involuntary or unfair.

➤ The source may be unreliable. A risk assessment from a company that makes or uses the substance in question is likely to be biased. But beware of bias and hype from all parties.

Fallacy: *Government testing proves that food is rarely contaminated with dangerous levels of pesticides or drugs.*

Fact: About 1 percent of domestically grown food and 3 percent of imported food tested contain illegal residues. However, the FDA doesn't regularly test fruits, vegetables, and grains for half the pesticides that could be present.[8] The USDA is even worse: the tests it uses on meat and poultry detect fewer than 20 percent of the pesticides that the USDA itself considers of potential concern.[9] Even the foods found to contain illegal residues usually reach the market anyway.[10] Not only that, the allowable levels for many pesticides, veterinary drugs, and other contaminants are probably too high, because they were established before research uncovered the potential health risks of these substances.

Fallacy: *The latest study is the most reliable evidence of whether a chemical is safe or dangerous.*

Fact: You can suffer mental whiplash if you base your actions on every "latest" study. Don't think that the first or most recent study is completely reliable just because it got a headline in today's newspaper. Most problems are sufficiently subtle that one study isn't enough to establish with confidence that a chemical is safe or dangerous.

Fallacy: *Using pesticides is the only practical way to feed our country. Growing food organically is just too expensive.*

Fact: Try telling that to Fred Kirschenmann, who successfully farms 3,000 acres organically in North Dakota; or Rex Spray, who's been farming 800 acres in Ohio without pesticides for 15 years—or any of the thousands of other farmers who produce for the booming organic food market, which was valued at $1.25 billion in 1989 and is growing at the rate of 30 percent annually.

Organic food generally costs more right now, because it's still a specialty item. But speaking of costs: What's the cost of cleaning up Iowa's shallow wells, half of which are contaminated by pesticides? What's the cost of pesticide-related illness and death to farmers and farm workers? What's the cost of developing new pesticides as the pests become resistant to the old ones? Considering these very real costs of using pesticides, organic food begins to look like a bargain.

Fallacy: *Food additives and pesticide residues are not worth worrying about because other risks are far greater.*

Fact: True, the risks from cigarette smoking, alcohol, and unsafe sex dwarf the dangers from pesticides in food. But the important difference is this: we have some control over whether we smoke, drink, or engage in unsafe sex; we don't have control over whether the apple in the supermarket is tainted with dangerous pesticides. Food safety is supposed to be the government's job. And the existence of one problem doesn't mean we can afford to ignore the others. Should we stop building safety features on lawn mowers, for example, just because cigarettes kill more people?

FIVE STEPS TO SAFER FOOD

Here are some of the most important things you can do to make sure your food is the safest food possible. Each of these steps will be discussed in detail in the chapters that follow.

1. Eat a nutritious diet. Avoiding pesticides and additives in food won't protect you from heart disease and cancer if you still consume too much fat and cholesterol, sodium, and alcohol; eat too few fruits, vegetables, and whole grains; or if you smoke cigarettes—all of which pose greater risks to your health. The first step to reducing food-related risks is to take a good, hard look at your diet, and start making any necessary changes today. (For practical suggestions on eating a more nutritious diet, see "Nutrition: Safe Food/Healthy Food," page 23.)

2. Choose safe food. If you eat meat, poultry, or fish, choose the leanest meat and the least fatty fish varieties. (Breast of turkey and chicken, pork tenderloin, round steak, and sirloin are leanest. Even "lean" and "extra lean" ground beef are not really lean—more than half of their calories come from fat.)

Preferably before cooking, remove all the visible fat from meat and fish, and the skin from fish and poultry. You'll be cutting down your fat intake, as well as reducing your exposure to the pesticides and other chemicals that accumulate in fatty tissues. If possible, buy meat that is produced without the routine use of antibiotics and other drugs.

And choose fish caught far from shore, including cod, haddock, and pollock, which are less likely to be contaminated with chemicals than those caught close to shore or in fresh water. One exception is salmon, an excellent source of good-for-your-heart omega-3 fatty acids. Despite being a high-fat fish caught close to shore, it's usually safe.

Choose locally grown, certified organic, and minimally processed foods as often as possible. Whenever you can, buy locally grown produce in season—it is fresher and often better tasting than other produce, and is almost never coated with wax and post-harvest pesticides. For produce grown without synthetic pesticides, seek out certified organic fruit and vegetables. New federal legislation will soon help to ensure that food labeled "organically grown" really is. (See "What does 'organic' mean?" page 53.) By choosing unprocessed or minimally processed foods, you can avoid the extra fat, sodium, or sugar typically added to processed foods, as well as potentially harmful food additives.

3. Buy food fresh and store it properly. Observe expiration or "use-by" or "sell-by" dates on foods such as dairy products, eggs, meat, and poultry. Buy fish with bright, shiny flesh and skin.

And keep food properly refrigerated. Assume that milk, eggs, cheese, fish, meat, and poultry are contaminated with harmful bacteria. Keeping these foods cold stops most types of bacteria from multiplying to possibly dangerous levels. Don't leave these foods out for more than two hours. Thaw food overnight in your refrigerator, instead of at room temperature, which allows bacteria to thrive.

4. Handle and prepare food safely. Wash fruits and vegetables thoroughly. This can help remove some (though not all) of the pesticide residues, as well as harmful bacteria that might be present on the food. Remove outer leaves from leafy vegetables, and peel produce when appropriate. (For tips on when to peel and not to peel, see page 69.)

Cook eggs, meat, fish, and poultry thoroughly to kill harmful bacteria that may be present. Use care with these foods to avoid "cross-contamination"—spreading bacteria to other foods. After handling raw eggs, meat, fish, and poultry, wash your hands, utensils, and kitchen surfaces with hot, soapy water. Bacteria and viruses in food cause thousands of deaths each year.

5. Demand a safer marketplace. With some food-safety problems, you can do very little on your own to reduce your risks, but making your views known in concert with others can make a difference. With some hazards, the risks to one individual may be minimal, but when multiplied by 250 million people, the risks to society as a whole may well be high enough to warrant action by government or industry. The best way to bring about that action is for enough people to demand it. We'll tell you how!

Defensive eating

Eating safely calls for particular vigilance if you are over 60, if you are HIV-positive or have AIDS, liver disease, cancer, are on chemotherapy, or have a weakened immune system.

If you're pregnant or breast-feeding, you can do several things to protect your baby from chemical contaminants and certain food-borne bacteria. (However, the advice in this book should not substitute for the advice of your physician.)

If you are over 60, or are HIV-positive or have AIDS, liver disease, cancer, or a weak immune system:

◆ Never drink unpasteurized (raw) milk, or eat raw or undercooked shellfish, eggs, poultry, fish, or meat. Partially cooked hamburgers, rare roast beef, and dishes made with raw or lightly cooked eggs— such as homemade eggnog, ice cream, and Caesar salad dressing—may increase your risk of bacterial infection. Resist the temptation to nibble uncooked cookie dough containing raw eggs. Be especially careful when handling raw poultry, meat, and eggs. Follow the detailed steps in Chapters 3, 4, and 5 on handling these foods properly.

◆ Be careful when traveling in foreign countries. Don't buy food from street vendors. Avoid salads and raw vegetables, peel your own fruit, and only eat cooked food that's still hot. Drink only boiled or bottled water, and use ice cubes made only from boiled water.

◆ Avoid soft cheeses such as Mexican-style cheese, Brie, and Camembert, which may be contaminated with listeria. People with AIDS are 200 to 300 times more susceptible to listeriosis than most other people are.

If you're pregnant:

◆ Follow the steps above, because some bacterial infections can be harmful to fetuses. Listeria is particularly dangerous for fetuses.

◆ Cook meat and fish thoroughly, not only to kill bacteria, but also to kill the parasite that causes toxoplasmosis. Infants who acquire the parasite from their mothers before birth can face severe health hazards, such as mental retardation. If you have outdoor cats, wear gloves when you work in the garden. Cats can be carriers of toxoplasmosis, which is why someone else should change the cat litter box while you're pregnant.

◆ Include in your diet only certain fish, in order to minimize risks to your developing baby. For example, to avoid exposing the fetus to dangerous levels of mercury, don't eat swordfish, shark, or marlin, and limit yourself to one-half pound per week of tuna. Also avoid eating fish contaminated with PCBs—fish from the Great Lakes and Hudson River are apt to be contaminated, as are many freshwater fish from other inland waterways. Fish likely to contain high levels of PCBs include freshwater carp, wild catfish, lake trout, whitefish, bluefish, mackerel, and striped bass.

◆ Choose low-fat fish and meats, and trim meat of fat. Pesticides and PCBs accumulate in fat.

◆ To avoid any possibility of contaminating food with lead, store fruit juice and acidic foods in glass or plastic containers. Don't use leaded crystal or ceramic containers, especially imported or handcrafted ceramics. Choose seamless or welded-seam cans instead of soldored-seam cans, which may have lead (see page 178). Don't use warm tap water for drinking or cooking, and consider getting your water tested if you suspect that lead might be present (see page 133).

◆ Avoid alcohol, caffeine, and the flavoring quinine.

If you're breast-feeding:

◆ Follow the steps above on choosing safe fish and avoiding lead, because babies are particularly vulnerable to PCBs and toxic metals. See page 146 to see if you should consider testing your breast milk for contaminants.

◆ Be aware that if you drink alcohol or caffeine, it may be passed to your baby through breast milk.

BUGS, DRUGS, AND MORE

The food risks we face can be broken down into six general categories. Here's an overview of food-safety problems and what you can do about them. The remaining chapters of *Safe Food* discuss these problems and solutions in more detail.

BACTERIA, VIRUSES, AND PARASITES

Food-borne microorganisms cause as many as 80 million cases of intestinal illness every year in the United States[11] and kill about 9,000 people annually. Most vulnerable are people whose immune systems are undeveloped or impaired—such as infants, the elderly, people who are HIV-positive, or people who have AIDS or cancer.

Almost any food can be contaminated with disease-causing bacteria. Crowded conditions in large-scale, factory-like farms and insanitary processing practices may contribute to the spread of bacteria in meat and poultry. Poultry is frequently contaminated with bacteria. Surveys show that up to 90 percent of retail raw chickens are contaminated with salmonella or other bacteria.[12] Eggs may also be contaminated—in fact, contaminated eggs were linked to 82 percent of the food-poisoning outbreaks between 1985 and 1989 that were caused by one type of bacterium, *Salmonella enteritidis*.[13] (Generally, an "outbreak" of food poisoning affects more than one person.) Improperly cooked meat may also harbor dangerous parasites, such as trichinella in pork. And improperly treated sewage may contribute to bacterial and viral contamination in fish—particularly in raw shellfish.

Safe Food solutions

◆ Handle food carefully and cook food thoroughly to kill microorganisms and stop them from spreading or contaminating other food.

◆ Demand that the government require that animals be raised and slaughtered in ways that minimize the chances for disease and contamination, step up food-inspection programs to help control microbial contamination, and do a better job of controlling water pollution from sewage. (See page 130.)

PESTICIDES, INDUSTRIAL CHEMICALS, AND TOXIC METALS

Because of their widespread use in agriculture and industry, pesticides, industrial chemicals, and heavy metals can be anywhere—in air, soil, water, and food. Some heavy metals occur naturally, too. Agricultural run-off and industrial dumping may lead to contamination in fish and shellfish. Any food may be contaminated with pesticides.

Unlike the effects of harmful bacteria, which are usually evident within a few hours or a few weeks, the effects of exposure to chemical or industrial contaminants usually don't appear for years or even decades. Individually, some of the chemicals that may contaminate food are carcinogenic (cancer-causing) or neurotoxic (nerve-damaging), or may cause other chronic human health problems. Children may be particularly vulnerable, in part because their bodies' defense mechanisms are not fully developed. No one knows for sure how much illness may be caused by the long-term, cumulative exposure to these chemicals, alone or in combination with one another.

Safe Food solutions

◆ You can reduce your exposure to some—though not all—pesticides by washing produce, trimming fat off

Foods to avoid

➤ **raw shellfish** (oysters, mussels, and clams)
problems: bacteria, viruses, toxic metals

➤ **undercooked poultry and meat**
problem: bacteria

➤ **raw milk**
problem: bacteria

➤ **raw eggs** and dishes containing raw eggs (such as homemade eggnog and Caesar salad dressing)
problem: bacteria

➤ **certain large fish** (large salmon and trout caught in the Great Lakes or polluted rivers, and large bluefish)
problems: PCBs, pesticides

➤ **over-done, grilled fatty meats**
problems: PAHs, HAs, pesticides, and fat

➤ **food in lead-soldered cans; food stored in lead crystal or ceramics that leach lead**
problem: lead

➤ **moldy peanuts and corn**
problem: aflatoxin

You may be surprised by the prominence of microbiological problems on this list. The reason is that microbes can cause immediate sickness or death that can be traced to particular foods. Pesticides, drugs, additives, and contaminants may cause cancer, behavioral and other effects, but these kinds of health problems can rarely be linked directly to particular foods.

meat and fish, and eating low-fat meals. You can also reduce your pesticide intake by seeking out certified organic foods, and fish from waters that are unpolluted. (See pages 68 and 128.)

◆ Demand that the government ban dangerous pesticides, tighten regulations on allowable pesticide and other contaminant levels, improve monitoring and enforcement, control and clean up pollution, and support farming methods that reduce pesticide use. (See page 75.)

NATURAL TOXINS

A variety of naturally occurring chemicals may cause cancer, illness, or, rarely, death. Some of these toxins, such as aflatoxin, are produced by mold in grains, nuts, and peanuts. Suspected cancer-causing chemicals, including PAHs (polycyclic aromatic hydrocarbons), are created when fatty foods are smoked or grilled; others, such as HAs (heterocyclic amines), form most readily when meat, poultry, or fish is pan-fried or boiled until overdone. Certain fish may contain toxins such as ciguatoxin; shellfish may contain toxins such as paralytic shellfish toxin. Some foods, including comfrey tea or false morels (a type of wild mushroom), contain naturally occurring substances that may cause cancer; other foods may develop toxins if they're stored improperly, such as the nerve poison solanine in green potatoes.

Safe Food solutions

◆ Avoid the foods that are most likely to contain natural toxins. Never eat moldy nuts and grains. Avoid comfrey, coltsfoot, and false morels. Cut out and throw away green or damaged spots on potatoes. And don't eat noncommercially harvested shellfish. Although ciguatoxin, scombrotoxin, or paralytic shellfish toxin can't be detected by smell or taste or destroyed by cooking, the risks are mainly associated with certain regions of the

17

country or certain types of seafood, so avoiding them is relatively easy. (See page 120.)

◆ Cook food in ways to minimize formation of PAHs and HAs. (See page 111.)

◆ Urge the government to tighten limits on the presence of toxins such as aflatoxin, and establish a mandatory seafood-safety program that would, among other things, ensure that fish don't contain dangerous levels of natural toxins. (See page 130.)

VETERINARY DRUGS

Many foods—including milk, meat, poultry, and farm-raised fish—may contain traces of antibiotics and other veterinary drugs. Veterinary drugs are used widely in food animals—both legally and illegally—to combat disease and stress, especially on factory-type farms, where overcrowding is the norm. While many of these veterinary drugs can be safely used, some are carcinogenic and others may cause allergies in humans. Routine use of antibiotics promotes the proliferation of antibiotic-resistant bacteria, thereby reducing the effectiveness of antibiotics in treating human disease.

Safe Food solutions

◆ Buy meat and poultry produced without the routine use of drugs. (See page 106.)

◆ Urge the government to improve its testing for drug residues in milk and other foods; stop the use of illegal, dangerous, or unnecessary veterinary drugs; support farming methods that avoid confinement and overcrowding; and rely less on veterinary drugs in general. (See page 97.)

FOOD ADDITIVES

Most processed foods contain additives, such as colorings and flavorings, emulsifiers, and thickening agents.

Although most of these additives are harmless, and a number are even good for you (see Chapter 7), some (such as sulfites) can cause fatal allergic reactions, and others (such as BHA) may increase slightly your risk of cancer. Other additives have not been tested well enough to guarantee their safety. Many food additives are unnecessary. Artificial colors and flavors, for example, are often used together to substitute for more expensive and more nutritious fruits or other natural ingredients.

If you suspect food poisoning

Some experts at the FDA estimate that almost every American suffers a food-borne illness over the span of a year or two. The symptoms of food poisoning vary. The symptoms of bacterial infection usually show up any time between two hours to two days after eating contaminated food. The tingling, numbness, and other neurological symptoms of food poisoning from some toxins in fish can occur immediately. And symptoms of botulism poisoning, including fatigue and blurred vision, may take as long as a week to show up. Here's what you should do if you suspect food poisoning:

◆ Seek treatment if the symptoms are severe, or if the victim is a child, a pregnant woman, an elderly person, or someone with a chronic illness.

◆ Drink plenty of liquids (such as water, apple juice, tea, or bouillon) to replace those lost through vomiting and diarrhea.

◆ Save the packaging and the remaining suspect food, if possible. This can help authorities to track down the problem, and may prevent other people from getting sick. Store the food in the freezer in a heavy plastic bag labeled "Danger, don't eat!" Write down the name of the food, when it was consumed, and the date of the illness.

◆ Call your local health department if the food is a commercial product, was prepared and packaged in a retail grocery store, or was from a restaurant, deli, or other commercial establishment.

Safe Food solutions

◆ Check processed food labels for the presence of harmful additives. (See page 158.)

◆ Demand that the government ban unsafe additives. (See page 169.)

ALLERGENS AND OTHER SUBSTANCES

Although harmless to most people, certain foods or food additives can cause allergic or other reactions ranging from mild rashes to difficulty breathing or even death. Milk, eggs, wheat, and peanuts are among the most common causes of food allergies. In addition, some chemicals added to food may target the brain or nervous system and cause a mental or behavioral effect, such as depression or anxiety. For example, some people report physical and behavioral reactions to monosodium glutamate (MSG), a flavoring used in sauces and soups. Many people also believe that aspartame, an artificial sweetener in diet soft drinks and other foods, is responsible for their headaches, hallucinations, and other problems. Other additives that have caused allergic or other reactions include Yellow No. 5 dye, which is used in processed foods and medicines; psyllium, used in cereal and Metamucil; and sulfites, which may be in wine, shrimp, and cut potatoes.

Safe Food solutions

◆ Avoid foods and other substances that may be causing reactions; check labels and question restaurant managers.

◆ Look for companies, such as Special Foods, that carry products for people with food allergies or sensitivities. To obtain a mail-order catalog from Special Foods, write to them at 9207 Shotgun Court, Springfield, VA 22153.

◆ Demand that the government ban sulfites and other food additives discovered to cause severe reactions. Urge your city or state government to require chain restaurants to provide ingredient information on packages or in brochures, and other restaurants to provide ingredient listings to customers who ask for them.

◆ Join organizations that provide information on avoiding or eliminating offending substances. (See page 209.)

WHO PROTECTS OUR FOOD?

Several government agencies are charged with the responsibility for safeguarding our food supply. Use this list as a guide to the regulatory agencies mentioned throughout *Safe Food* and as an action guide for your own use. (You'll find the addresses of these agencies in Chapter 10.)

The FDA

The Food and Drug Administration (FDA) is responsible for ensuring the "safety and wholesomeness" of all food sold in interstate commerce except meat, poultry, and eggs. (See USDA below.) Part of the Department of Health and Human Services, the FDA has primary responsibility for regulating food additives. It also regulates veterinary drugs and sets "tolerance levels," or maximum legal limits, for drug residues in milk, eggs, and raw meat and poultry, as well as some limits on chemical contaminants in fish. The FDA is also responsible for enforcing limits on pesticide residues in food, and tests food (except meat and poultry) for pesticide residues and other contaminants. The FDA also regulates the labeling of food, except meat, poultry, eggs, and alcoholic beverages.

The USDA

The U.S. Department of Agriculture (USDA) is responsible for the safety of meat, poultry, and eggs sold through interstate commerce. The USDA's Food Safety and Inspection Service (FSIS) is responsible for inspecting meat and poultry products, and regulates food and color additives in meat and poultry. The USDA's Agricultural Marketing Service (AMS) inspects eggs and egg products, and has been assigned the lead role in implementing newly required national standards for organic food.

The EPA

The Environmental Protection Agency (EPA) is responsible for approving the use and application levels of pesticides and setting tolerance levels for pesticide residues in foods. These levels are enforced by the FDA. The EPA sets national drinking-water standards for public drinking water supplies. The FDA regulates bottled water based on EPA standards.

Other federal agencies

Part of the U.S. Department of Commerce, the National Marine Fisheries Service offers a voluntary, fee-for-service fish-inspection program that covers about 10 percent of the seafood consumed in the United States every year.[14] Currently, there is no mandatory federal fish-inspection program.

The Bureau of Alcohol, Tobacco and Firearms, a division of the Treasury Department, oversees the labeling of alcoholic beverages and regulates the use of FDA-approved additives in alcoholic beverages.

State and local governments

State and local governments have the primary responsibility for monitoring milk and dairy products for bacteria and antibiotics, and testing eggs for salmonella. States also regulate the safety of food not sold in interstate commerce. Twenty-nine states and the District of Columbia participate in the National Shellfish Sanitation Program, which monitors oysters, clams, and mussels for contamination and closes unsafe waters to harvesting. About half of the states also have their own meat and poultry inspection programs, and many states have monitoring programs for pesticides in produce. Local governments enforce health and labeling requirements in supermarkets and restaurants.

NUTRITION: SAFE FOOD/HEALTHY FOOD

Safe eating doesn't just mean avoiding pesticides or food poisoning—it also means choosing the right foods for a healthy diet. After decades of research and debate, government and other health experts are in general agreement about the relationship between diet and chronic diseases. Ironically, while past nutrition policy in the United States focused on ensuring that people ate enough food, today the problem for most people is eating too much.

For example, plenty of evidence shows that too much saturated fat and cholesterol in the diet causes coronary heart disease and stroke. Too much fat of any kind may lead to obesity, cancers of the breast and colon, and diabetes. Too much sodium is linked to high blood pressure and stroke. Too much alcohol may cause liver cirrhosis, cancer of the mouth and throat, birth defects, high blood pressure, and brain damage. Too much sugar can lead to tooth decay and, possibly, obesity. And too many refined foods instead of fiber-rich and vitamin-rich vegetables, fruits, and whole grains may cause constipation and diverticulosis, and promote cancer of the colon and coronary heart disease.

Fortunately, a very enjoyable, varied and flavorful diet can also be low in fat, cholesterol, salt, and sugar, while providing plenty of fiber, protein, vitamins, and minerals. First, though, you may have to unlearn what you were once taught about nutrition. Remember "balance, variety, and moderation"? That advice was vague enough to include practically anything. You could meet the old "basic four" requirement with a greasy hamburger with lettuce and cheese on a bun. (See page 28 for a new, healthier take on the "basic four" food groups—and clear advice on how much of each kind of food you should be eating and what to avoid.)

Here are some of the most important goals of a nutritious diet—and some practical tips for reaching these goals:

Eat less fat, saturated fat, and cholesterol. If you decide to make just one change in your diet, let this be it. Americans typically consume about 40 percent of their calories from fat. The American Heart Association, the National Cancer Institute, and other agencies all recommend that anyone over the age of two consume no more than 30 percent of calories from fat, and only a third of those from saturated fat. (Lots of artery-clogging saturated fat is found in meat, cheese, whole milk, ice cream, and processed foods containing coconut oil, palm-kernel oil, butter, beef fat, palm oil, and lard.) The American Health Foundation and CSPI advise adults that maintaining a fat intake of 20 percent of calories or less would be even better. Furthermore, the less saturated fat and cholesterol you consume, the better. Cutting your cholesterol intake from 450 milligrams to about 250 to 300 milligrams a day could lower your blood cholesterol by 10 points. Egg yolks, meat, and dairy products are the major sources of cholesterol in a typical American diet.

Chapter 10 includes good sources of information on reducing the fat, saturated fat, and cholesterol in your diet, and the chart at the end of this chapter will also help you "cut that fat." Buying yourself a good low-fat/low-cholesterol cookbook might be one of the best investments you could make.

Meanwhile, probably the easiest way to reduce fat—other than counting every gram or teaspoon you consume—is to identify and cut back on the major sources. Spreads, dressings, and sauces such as butter, margarine, mayonnaise, salad dressings, oils, and shortenings, which provide about 10 percent of the fat in a typical diet, are the easiest to eliminate, since they are visibly added to other foods. When hidden within cakes, cookies, chips, fries, and frozen dinners, however, fats are much harder to control. But it's the fat in meat, poultry, and fish that makes up most—more than 40 percent—of our fat intake. You can cut some of this fat away, but the rest is in the food itself. The fat in dairy foods, including milk, ice cream, and cheese, probably makes up another 15 to 20 percent of your fat consumption. You can reduce your fat intake significantly by eating less of these foods and choosing low-fat or nonfat varieties. The remainder of the fat in a typical diet comes from foods such as nuts, seeds, and eggs. **How to cut back on fat:**

◆ Drink skim or 1 percent low-fat milk (2 percent isn't really low-fat) instead of whole milk, and choose nonfat or low-fat yogurt and low-fat cheeses.

◆ Eat less red meat. Substitute beans, pasta, rice, potatoes, vegetables, and low-fat cottage cheese, fish, and chicken without the skin. Avoid hot dogs, bologna, and most other luncheon meats—fat provides about 80 percent of their calories. Try your hand at low-fat versions of cuisines from around the world—Chinese, Mexican, Middle Eastern, Greek, Italian—which combine vegetables and grains with smaller amounts of meat or no meat at all.

◆ When you do eat meat, cut off as much fat as possible, both before and after you cook it. Remember that "Choice" and "Prime" cuts are highest in fat; "Select" grade is lower in fat, cheaper, and perfectly acceptable.

◆ Check the fat content on ingredient labels—don't rely on claims that a product is 90 percent or 95 percent "fat free," "light" or "lite," or even that it has "less fat." As a rough rule of thumb, about 3 grams of fat or less per serving is low in fat, and more than 10 grams is high.

To calculate the actual percentage of fat calories in a product, first multiply the grams of fat per serving by 9— the number of calories in a gram of fat. That equals the number of fat calories in a serving. Divide that number by the total calorie count per serving, and multiply by 100. For example, a serving of whole milk contains 8 grams of fat and 150 total calories: 8 times 9 equals 72, divided by 150, equals .48, times 100, equals 48 percent fat calories. The goal is to choose a variety of foods that average no more than 20 percent of calories from fat overall. Thus, some foods might be 30 percent or more, while others will be 10 percent or less.

◆ Eat your bread plain, or switch to all-fruit jam, nonfat or low-fat yogurt, or apple butter instead of butter, margarine, or cream cheese.

◆ For dessert, eat fresh fruit, low-fat frozen yogurt, fat-free frozen desserts, ice milk, or fat-free cakes or cookies instead of doughnuts, pies, pastries, cakes, or ice cream, which are high in fat.

◆ Poach or steam vegetables, fish, and other foods instead of frying or sautéing them. If you do sauté, use olive oil—it's not low in fat, but it is low in saturated fat and doesn't appear to promote cancer.

◆ Use reduced-calorie and fat-free salad dressings and mayonnaise.

◆ Use canned tuna packed in water rather than oil.

◆ When cooking with eggs, discard half or more of the yolks (which contain all the cholesterol in eggs) and enjoy a lighter, healthier omelette or soufflé.

Cut back on your salt (sodium) intake. The less sodium you consume, the better. Most Americans consume as much as 4,000 to 6,000 milligrams of sodium per day. The National Academy of Sciences recommends cutting this level to 2,400 milligrams as an interim goal for adults, and ideally cutting back to 1,800 milligrams—less than a teaspoon of salt a day. (Pregnancy increases the need for sodium, however, so don't cut way back if you're pregnant.) Although most foods naturally contain some sodium, about 90 percent of the sodium we consume comes from added salt—most of it in processed foods. But high-sodium foods don't necessarily taste salty. A McDonald's iced-cheese Danish contains almost three times as much sodium as a medium order of French fries. A one-ounce serving of Total breakfast cereal contains more than twice the sodium as an ounce of Fritos.

Unsalted food doesn't mean bland food. Once you become accustomed to fresh foods without (or with less) added salt, you'll be surprised how good real food can taste. **How to cut back on salt:**

◆ Eat unprocessed foods.

◆ Read processed food labels carefully and choose brands with less sodium. For example, Healthy Choice, Eating Right, and Snoopy's Choice frozen entrees and meals have far less sodium than most others, including Lean Cuisine, Budget Gourmet Light, and Le Menu Light Style.

◆ Season foods with pepper, curry, garlic, and other spices and herbs instead of salt. Or buy a salt substitute, such as Mrs. Dash. (Sea salt has just as much sodium as regular table salt.) Season vegetables and fish with lemon juice instead of salt.

◆ Substitute reduced-sodium soy sauce for regular soy sauce, and use it sparingly.

◆ Choose natural, not American and other processed cheeses, and fresh meats rather than their processed counterparts, such as hot dogs, luncheon meats, ham, and sausage.

◆ Rinse canned beans, vegetables, and fish to wash away some of the added salt.

The "Basic Four" revisited

Here's a new look at the old "basic four" food groups. Each group is divided into "Anytime," "Sometimes," and "Seldom" categories according to fat, cholesterol, salt, and/or sugar levels. The chart also tells you how many daily servings of each group you should eat. Wondering if you'll have time to do anything but eat bread and carrots all day? Relax. The servings are quite small (one slice

GRAIN GROUP

9 servings

Anytime

Whole-grain bread,* rolls,*
    bagels*
Whole-grain crackers,*[3] tortillas*
Brown rice*
Bulgur
Whole-grain breakfast cereal*
Pasta*

FRUIT & VEGETABLE GROUP

7 servings

Anytime

All fruits and vegetables (except
    those at right)
Applesauce, unsweetened
Potatoes, white or sweet

* Refined-grain versions have less fiber, vitamins, and minerals.

A healthy diet doesn't require eating meat, fish, poultry, eggs, or dairy products.
(See page 204 for some resources for vegetarians.)

of bread, one piece of fruit, or ½ cup of rice, pasta, or vegetables, for example). The chart works best if you compare foods within groups (whole milk vs. skim), not between groups (rice vs. hot dogs). In later chapters, you'll find out how to select, prepare, and store the nutritious foods of your choice to make sure they're as safe as possible.

Sometimes	Seldom
Muffins*[6]	Croissants[3]
Waffles, pancakes*[3]	Doughnuts[1,6]
Heavily sweetened cereals[6]	Danish[6]
Fat-free cakes[6]	Bread stuffing from mix[1,3]
Granola cereals	

Sometimes	Seldom
Avocado[2], guacamole[2]	Coconut[1]
Dried fruit	Pickles[3]
Canned fruit[6]	Scalloped or au gratin potatoes[1,3]
Fruit juice	
Vegetables, canned, with salt[3]	
French fries or hash browns, fried in vegetable oil[2]	

1 high in saturated fat
2 high in unsaturated fat
3 may be high in salt or sodium
4 high in cholesterol
5 may be rich in beneficial omega-3 fats
6 high in added sugar

Chart continues on next page

29

MILK GROUP

2 servings

Anytime
1% low-fat cottage cheese[3]
Dry-curd cottage cheese
Skim milk
1% low-fat milk
Nonfat yogurt

FISH, POULTRY, MEAT, EGGS, BEANS, & NUTS GROUP

2 servings

Fish
(5-oz. roasted)

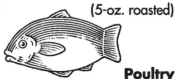

Anytime
All finfish[5]
Salmon, canned[3,5]
Sardines, in fish oil[3,5]
Tuna, water-pack[3]
Shellfish, except shrimp

Poultry
(4 ounces, roasted)

Chicken breast (without skin)
Turkey breast, drumstick, thigh
Ground turkey (without skin)

Red meats
(3 ounces, trimmed
and roasted)

Pork tenderloin
Eye of the round
Top round

Eggs

Egg white

Beans, peas, & nuts

Beans, peas, lentils

Sometimes

2% low-fat or regular cottage cheese[3]
Reduced-fat or part-skim cheeses[3]
2% low-fat milk
Low-fat yogurt, plain or fruit[6]
Ice milk or nonfat ice cream[6]
Frozen nonfat or low-fat yogurt[6]

Seldom

Hard cheeses (like cheddar)[1,3]
Processed cheeses[1,3]
Whole milk[1]
Whole-milk yogurt[1]
Ice cream[1,6]

Sometimes

Fried fish[2]
Sardines, in vegetable oil[3]
Tuna, oil-pack
Shrimp[4]

Chicken breast (with skin)
Chicken drumstick, thigh
Fried chicken (except thigh)[2]
Ground turkey (with skin)

Bottom round steak, sirloin steak
Lean ham[3]
Pork or lamb loin chop
Leg of lamb, veal sirloin
Veal loin or rib chop

Tofu[2], peanut butter[2], nuts[2]

Seldom

Fried chicken thigh[2] or wing[2]
Chicken hot dog[3]

Chuck blade[1], rib roast[1]
Extra-lean or lean ground beef[1]
Pork or lamb[1] rib chop, bacon
Bologna[1,3], salami[1,3], hot dog[1,3]
Any untrimmed red meat[1]

Whole egg or yolk[4]

1 high in saturated fat
2 high in unsaturated fat
3 may be high in salt or sodium

4 high in cholesterol
5 may be rich in beneficial omega-3 fats
6 high in added sugar

◆ Skip the salt when you cook rice, hot cereal, pasta, and frozen vegetables.

◆ Avoid canned soups that are too salty. Make your own broth from vegetable peelings and trimmed meats, or use canned broth or bouillon made without salt.

Eat more fiber-rich and vitamin-rich foods. For many years, dietary fiber was dismissed as "roughage" and was considered of more value in livestock feed than in human diets. But in the 1970s, Denis Burkitt, M.D., a British physician, began a crusade to restore fiber to its rightful place in the diet. He said that dietary fiber could prevent everything from constipation and diverticulosis to colon cancer.

Burkitt based his claims both on medical studies and on his own experiences in Africa. His native patients obtained huge amounts of fiber from their traditional foods, whereas his European and westernized native patients ate relatively refined foods that provided little fiber. Burkitt noticed that the high-fiber-eating natives had low rates of numerous illnesses that were common afflictions of Europeans and natives who had adopted European diets.

Research shows that populations that include more whole grains in their diets have lower rates of colon cancer, and populations that consume more vegetables and fruits have lower risks of cancers of the lung, mouth, esophagus, stomach, and colon. Scientists aren't sure whether it's the fiber or other constituents that are responsible. Animal studies suggest that the fiber, beta-carotene, and vitamin C in these foods all may protect against cancer.

The National Cancer Institute recommends doubling or tripling daily fiber intake from 10 grams to 20 or 30 grams. Fiber-rich foods include canned or cooked dried beans and peas (such as black, kidney, pinto, navy, great northern, and garbanzo beans; split and black-eyed peas; and lentils), whole-grain breads and cereals, and vegetables and fruits. **How to boost your fiber:**

◆ Add garbanzo beans to salads. Try vegetarian chili, and lentil, split pea, or other bean soups. Heat up canned black beans as a side dish.

◆ Try ethnic foods such as bean enchiladas (Mexican), humus (Middle Eastern), dal (Indian), and pasta e fagioli (Italian).

◆ Eat at least four servings of cooked or raw vegetables, and three servings of fruit each day. One serving is one-half cup, or one piece of fruit. Citrus and orange fruits (for example, cantaloupe, apricots, peaches, and oranges) and orange or green-leafy vegetables (sweet potatoes, broccoli, kale, carrots) are the richest in carotenes and vitamin C. Cabbage-family vegetables (including broccoli, cauliflower, and Brussels sprouts) have other constituents that might prevent cancer.

◆ Use cooked barley or bulgur instead of rice in pilafs, stuffings, soups, and stews.

◆ Substitute whole-wheat or spinach pasta for regular.

◆ Add wheat bran, wheat germ, or berries to cereals and pancake, waffle, or muffin batters.

◆ Substitute whole-wheat flour for white flour in baking. And choose whole-wheat or other whole-grain breads and crackers.

◆ Check labels—look for the words "whole-wheat" in the ingredients; if "wheat flour" or "enriched wheat flour" is listed, it's not whole-wheat bread.

Tame your sugar impulses. The average American eats about 100 pounds of sugar a year. Besides causing tooth decay, sugar is a problem because it provides "empty" calories.

The sheer volume of sugar that people consume substitutes for food with vitamins, minerals, fiber, and other needed nutrients. Sugar is often accompanied by fat in foods such as cakes, pastries, pies, cookies, ice cream, and chocolate. **How to cut back on sugar:**

◆ Look at labels of processed foods and stay away from those with sugar high on the list of ingredients. Check labels for different names for sugar, such as sucrose, dextrose, corn syrup, fructose, high-fructose corn syrup, brown sugar, molasses, and honey.

◆ Try decreasing the amount of sugar called for in recipes by one-quarter to one-third.

◆ Watch out for soft drinks, the greatest source of sugar in the American diet. Each 12-ounce can contains 9 to 10 teaspoons of refined sugar.

◆ Eat fresh fruit instead of sweet snacks or desserts —you'll be getting less sugar, and more vitamins, minerals, and fiber.

◆ Don't buy canned fruit, unless no fresh fruit is available. If you must buy it in cans, choose fruit packed in juice instead of syrup.

◆ Don't just substitute honey for the sugar in your diet. Honey has no nutrients to speak of and still promotes tooth decay. (It does have the advantage of being slightly sweeter than sugar, though, so you may use a little less of it. And in baking it provides moisture so that you can use a little less oil or shortening.) Brown sugar, raw sugar, and other "health food" sugars are no better than regular sugar—don't be deceived into thinking they're health foods. And avoid artificial sweeteners like aspartame, acesulfame K, and saccharin. (See Chapter 7.)

If you drink alcohol, do so only in moderation. The *Dietary Guidelines for Americans* recommends that men limit alcohol consumption to no more than two cans of beer, two small glasses of wine, or two average cocktails per day, and that women consume no more than one drink a day. The distinction is mainly due to differences in average weight and proportion of body fat. Women trying to get pregnant—and their mates[15]—as well as pregnant women and nursing mothers should avoid alcohol altogether. If you're taking medications, it's also best not to drink.

GETTING YOUR KIDS TO EAT WELL

Just watch TV with your kids one Saturday morning, and you'll see the pressure that's put on children to eat all the wrong kinds of fatty, sugary, and salty foods. Here are some tips for tempting your child into healthier habits that can last a lifetime:

◆ Set a good example by eating healthy foods yourself.

◆ Discuss why many of the foods advertised on TV are unhealthy.

◆ Avoid buying junk food; if there isn't any in the house, you can honestly say so if your child asks for it. Keep a wide variety of nutritious foods in the house for every taste and occasion.

◆ Respect your child's tastes. Many kids don't like spicy foods or dishes such as casseroles in which various foods become indistinguishable. Try raw, steamed, blanched, or stir-fried veggies served individually instead. Your child might not like steamed broccoli, but might enjoy it raw with a low-fat yogurt dip.

◆ Make nutritious food attractive to your child. Cut up fruit, vegetables, and sandwiches in different ways, maybe with cookie cutters. Rename food if that helps: green beans could become turtle food, broccoli might be trees, greens might be dinosaur food, and salmon-pasta casserole could be iguana stew (remember, you're catering to your child's taste, not yours). Try a nutritious at-home "picnic" for lunch—complete with a lunch box or picnic basket and tablecloth on the floor.

◆ Be sure that serving sizes are appropriate. Some parents suggest that their children eat a bite of each kind of food for every year of age—two bites for two-year-olds, three for three-year-olds, and so on. Most importantly, keep mealtime fun. If your child perceives a power struggle is going on, you lose!

◆ Serve the most nutritious part of the meal (such as vegetables and salad) first, when kids are hungriest. If you serve everything at once, your children are bound to fill up on their favorites, which might not be the most nutritious. Give your children nutritious options. Ask them which kind of vegetable they'd like for supper—carrots or sweet potatoes, broccoli or spinach—not whether they'd like one.

◆ Late afternoon is a good time to give your children carrots, broccoli, or celery sticks. Or rinse a can of garbanzo, pinto, white, or navy beans and serve them up instead. Try to offer these snacks before your kids realize they're hungry, because by then they may have their own ideas about what they want. Be prepared for the "snack attack" by packing healthy snack items—such as apples, carrot sticks, whole-grain crackers, or bagels—when you leave home.

◆ Kids are more likely to eat a meal they helped prepare. This will undoubtedly require more of your time, but your child will be learning cooking skills and responsibility. Get the book *Kitchen Fun for Kids*, by Michael Jacobson and Laura Hill, Henry Holt and Co., 1991. (See page 205.)

◆ Even better, plant a garden with your child. Children really do eat what they grow. (See page 208 for some help getting started.)

◆ Cut up vegetables, fruit, and low-fat cheese and keep them on the bottom shelf of the refrigerator at your child's eye level. For healthy snacks for older children, you could keep sandwiches in the refrigerator.

◆ Older children can mix their own beverages using fruit juices and seltzer water. You might set a rule that teen-agers have to pay for soft drinks out of their own allowance.

◆ If your child rejects a food, don't make a fuss or state categorically that your child "hates broccoli," for instance. Instead, try offering that food another time, perhaps prepared differently. You may be pleasantly surprised.

WHAT YOU CAN DO AS A CITIZEN—FOR YOUR KIDS

Your child doesn't just eat and learn about food at home. Here are some steps you can take to ensure that school lunches are more nutritious, and that your children are exposed to sound information about food—not junk-food propaganda:

◆ Encourage your local school food service and school principal to serve more nutritious meals that eliminate nitrite, sulfites, artificial colorings, BHA, BHT, and other unnecessary or risky additives. Tell them what foods you'd like them to serve instead. If they tell you that the costs are too great, join with other parents to organize for change.

◆ Demand that schools replace junk food with healthy foods in school vending machines.

◆ Recommend that schools use a sound nutrition curriculum, such as one prepared by the American Health Foundation or American Cancer Society, which goes beyond the basic four food groups.

◆ Ask your school board to ban from the classroom any food-company educational materials that promote unhealthy products or poor nutrition, or that place brand awareness above nutritional awareness.

◆ Involve local civic organizations in improving television advertising geared to children. Publicize misleading ads or ones that encourage bad eating habits, and report them to the Children's Advertising Review Unit of the Council of Better Business Bureaus, 845 Third Avenue, New York, NY 10022.

Cut that fat

Here are 43 easy suggestions for cutting your total fat and saturated fat consumption. Remember that the average American gets about 40 percent of calories from fat, and 15 percent from saturated fat. We recommend that adults cut both total-fat and saturated-fat intake in half. For example, a 25-year-old woman should eat no more than 20 grams of saturated fat per day; the average woman needs to cut 20 grams a day to reach that goal. (Most children aged 2 to 18 need to cut total fat intake by one-quarter and saturated fat by one-third.)

To find out how many grams of fat and saturated fat you and your family need to eliminate from your daily diets, check the "fat goals" chart below. Then decide which of the following substitutions you prefer, and add up the savings until you reach your goals. Add up your saturated fat savings first, because cutting back in that department will probably bring your total down automatically.

Find your "fat goals:"

If you are between the ages of:	Try to cut: total fat (grams)	saturated fat (grams)
children:		
2–3	15	8
4–10	21	10
females:		
11–18	25	13
19–50	49	20
51+	42	17
males:		
11–14	28	14
15–18	33	17
19–50	65	25
51+	51	20

To cut your fat and saturated fat intake...

Try:	Instead of:	Total fat savings (g)	Saturated fat savings (g)
PREPARED FOOD			
Healthy Choice Salisbury Steak (11.5 oz) *fat: 7 g/saturated fat: NA*	Budget Gourmet Light Salisbury Steak (11.5 oz) *15 / NA*	6	NA
Kraft Eating Right Macaroni and Cheese (9 oz.) *8 / 3*	Stouffer's Macaroni and Cheese (12 oz.) *26 / NA*	18	NA
Snoopy's Choice Macaroni and Cheese w/Turkey Franks (8.5 oz.) *5 / 2*	Kid Cuisine Macaroni and Cheese w/Mini Franks (9 oz.) *15 / NA*	10	NA
Mrs. Paul's Light Haddock (5 oz.) *6 / NA*	Mrs. Paul's Crunchy Batter Fish Sticks (5 oz.) *15 / 3*	9	NA
Aunt Jemima Lite Healthy Waffles (2) *2 / NA*	Eggo or Nutri-Grain Waffles (2) *10 / NA*	8	NA
Lipton Cream of Mushroom Soup Cup (10 oz.) *5 / NA*	Campbell Chunky Cream of Mushroom Soup (10 oz.) *20 / NA*	15	NA
Kraft Creamy Italian Dressing (2 Tb.) *10 / NA*	Marie's Italian Garlic Dressing (2 Tb.) *21 / NA*	11	NA
DAIRY			
1% Lowfat milk (1 cup) *2 / 1.5*	Whole milk (1 cup) *8 / 5*	6	4
Philadelphia Light Cream Cheese (2 Tb.) *5 / 3*	Philadelphia Cream Cheese (regular) (2 Tb.) *10 / 5*	5	2
Lowfat 1% cottage cheese (½ cup) *1 / 1*	Regular cottage cheese (½ cup) *5 / 3*	4	3
Kraft Light Cheese (1.5 oz.) *8 / 5*	Kraft Cheese (regular) (1.5 oz.) *14 / 8*	6	3
Dannon Lowfat Fruit-on-the Bottom Blueberry Yogurt (1 cup) *3 / NA*	Whitney's Blueberry Yogurt (1 cup) *7 / NA*	4	3*

NA = Not available. * CSPI estimate. Numbers may not add up because of rounding.

Try:	Instead of:	Total fat savings (g)	Saturated fat savings (g)
Sealtest Fat-Free Ice Cream (¾ cup) **fat: 0/saturated fat: 0**	Breyer's Regular Ice Cream (¾ cup) 13 / NA	13	8*
Sara Lee Lights French Cheesecake (3.3 oz.) 4 / NA	Sara Lee French Cheesecake (3.5 oz.) 19 / NA	15	NA
MEAT, POULTRY, AND FISH			
Trimmed select sirloin (5 oz.) 9 / 4	Untrimmed select sirloin (5 oz.) 20 / 8	11	5
Chicken drumstick without skin (2) 5 / 1	Drumstick with skin (2) 12 / 3	7	2
Trimmed select bottom round steak (5 oz.) 9 / 3	Trimmed select chuck blade steak (5 oz.) 17 / 7	8	4
Ground turkey (5 oz.) 19 / 5	Lean ground beef (5 oz.) 27 / 11	7	5
Skinless turkey thigh and drumstick (5 oz.) 5 / 2	Skinless chicken thigh and drumstick (5 oz.) 12 / 3	7	2
Pork tenderloin (5 oz.) 7 / 2	Pork rib chop, trimmed (5 oz.) 22 / 8	15	5
Canadian bacon (2 oz.) 5 / 2	Regular bacon (2 oz.) 28 / 10	23	8
Weaver Turkey Breast (2 oz.) 1 / NA	Butterball Turkey Bologna (2 oz.) 12 / NA	11	4*
Oscar Mayer Baked Cooked Ham breast (2 oz.) 1 / 0.3	Oscar Mayer Bologna (2 oz.) 17 / 6	16	6
Louis Rich Turkey Frank (1) 9 / 3	Oscar Mayer Beef Frank (1) 13 / 6	5	3
Flounder (5 oz.) 2 / 0.5	Skinless chicken thigh (5 oz.) 15 / 4	13	4
Light tuna in water (3 oz.) 0.4 / 0.1	Tuna in oil (3 oz.) 7 / 1	7	1
FAST FOOD			
McDonald's Apple Bran Muffin (1) 0 / 0	McDonald's Iced Cheese Danish (1) 22 / 6	22	6
McDonald's Lean Deluxe 10 / NA	Quarter Pounder 21 / 8	11	4*

NA = Not available. * CSPI estimate. Numbers may not add up because of rounding.

Try:	Instead of:	Total fat savings (g)	Saturated fat savings (g)
McDonald's Vanilla Shake (1) **fat: 1/saturated fat:** 0.6	Burger King Vanilla Shake (1) 10 / 6	9	5
Burger King Chicken Tenders (6) 13 / 3	McDonald's Chicken McNuggets (6) 16 / 4	3	1
Domino's Large Cheese Pizza (2 sl.) 10 / 6	Pizza Hut Hand-Tossed Medium Cheese Pizza (1½ sl.) 15 / 10	5	5
Kentucky Fried Chicken Lite 'n Crispy Side Breast 12 / 3	Kentucky Fried Chicken Extra Tasty Crispy Side Breast 22 / 6	10	2
Dunkin' Donuts Blueberry Muffin (1) 8 / NA	Dunkin' Donuts Chocolate Croissant (1) 29 / NA	21	NA
McDonald's Lite Dressing (1 packet) 2 / 0.4	McDonald's Peppercorn Dressing (1 packet) 44 / 7	42	7
OTHER FOODS			
Peppermint Patty (1.5 oz.) 4 / NA	Hershey's Milk Chocolate bar (1.6 oz.) 14 / NA	10	6*
Doritos Light Cool Ranch or Light Nacho Chips (1 oz.) 4 / NA	Tostitos Tortilla Chips (1 oz.) 8 / NA	4	NA
Snyder's Old Fashioned Pretzels (1 oz.) 0 / 0	Lay's Regular Potato Chips (1 oz.) 10 / NA	10	NA
Ruffles Light Potato Chips (1 oz.) 6 / NA	Pringles Regular Potato Chips (1 oz.) 13 / NA	7	NA
Nabisco Teddy Grahams snacks (1 oz.) 4 / NA	Nabisco Striped Chips Ahoy! Cookies (1 oz.) 10 / 4	6	NA
Pepperidge Farm Brown 'N Serve French Rolls (½) 1 / NA	Pillsbury Crescent Dinner Rolls (2) 12 / NA	11	NA
Kraft Fat-Free Mayonnaise (1 Tb.) 0 / 0	Kraft Regular Mayonnaise (1 Tb.) 11 / 2	11	2
Margarine (1 Tb.) 11 / 2	Butter (1 Tb.) 11 / 7	0	5
Nucoa Heart Beat Margarine (1 Tb.) 3 / 0.4	Fleischmann's Margarine (1 Tb.) 11 / 2	8	2

CHAPTER 2
FRUIT, VEGETABLES, & GRAINS

FRUIT, VEGETABLES, & GRAINS

Nothing beats the taste of ripe, fresh fruits and vegetables in season—sweet, juicy melon in summer, a just-picked ear of corn, a succulent red tomato—this is what good eating is all about. And fresh foods are packed with more than just good taste. Your mother was right to tell you to eat your vegetables—vegetables, along with fruits and whole grains, are our best sources of vitamins and minerals, complex carbohydrates, and dietary fiber. Studies have even linked diets rich in these plant foods with lower risks of coronary heart disease and cancers of the lung, stomach, colon, and esophagus.[1]

Since fresh produce and whole grains are so important to a good diet, the last thing you want to worry about is whether there are doses of pesticides in the spinach you're serving with dinner, the whole-wheat toast you had for breakfast, or the orange you tucked into your child's lunch box. Unfortunately, though, there is reason to be concerned. Because American farmers rely too heavily on pesticides and the government fails to keep these pesticides out of our food supply, fruit, vegetables, and grains contaminated with potentially harmful pesticide residues can and do make their way onto our plates.

It's impossible to detect contaminants simply by looking at any given food item at the store. The presence of pesticide residues depends on many factors, including where the food was grown and under what weather conditions, how much of what pesticides were applied to the crop, the storage conditions, and how carefully the store chooses its suppliers.

But pesticides or not, it would be folly to stop eating fruit, vegetables, and grains. On the contrary, most of us need to eat much more of these foods. The answer is to minimize your exposure to pesticides that may be in them. This can be done in many ways, from more careful preparation of supermarket fare, to buying certified organically grown produce, to growing your own. (We'll discuss all three.)

In the long run, to have a safer food supply, food producers need to greatly reduce their reliance on potentially dangerous agricultural pesticides. Consumer pressure is already helping to push the country in that direction, and as the demand increases for food grown with fewer or no pesticides, the supply will increase and prices will fall. That will be good news for everyone— except the chemical companies.

PESTICIDES? NO THANKS!

It began in the 1940s with pesticides such as DDT, and it would become nothing less than a revolution in agriculture. Synthetic pesticides promised farmers better pest control, greater crop yields, and lower labor costs. And they delivered on most of their promises. Pesticide use increased dramatically. In the United States, the use of pesticides increased 33-fold since 1945.[2] But as early as the 1960s, with the publication of Rachel Carson's *Silent Spring*, we were also learning about some of the costs of the pesticide revolution.

Today, we have an even better picture of these costs. In the United States, farmers now use 845 million pounds of the nearly 3 billion pounds of active pesticide ingredients annually, at a direct cost of approximately $5 billion.[3] The indirect costs of pesticide use include human poisonings, harm to fish and wildlife, livestock losses, groundwater contamination, destruction of natural vegetation, and more pests resistant to pesticides—not to mention the costs of developing and implementing government regulations and monitoring. In 1991, David Pimentel, Ph.D., an agricultural scientist at Cornell University, calculated that these indirect costs come to at least $955 million annually, and are probably closer to $2 to $4 billion.[4]

When pesticides are used in agriculture, they end up in our food, in our air, in the soil, in the grains we feed to livestock, and in our water. Here's a look at some of the problems:

Environmental contamination. As the result of normal agricultural use, 46 pesticides—some of them known to cause cancer or other harmful health effects—have been discovered in the groundwater in 26 states.[5] A recent EPA survey estimates that 10 percent of community and 4 percent of rural drinking water wells contain one or more pesticides, although most are below EPA's "safe" levels.[6]

Environmental groups have criticized EPA's testing, however. "EPA's testing for pesticides where we wouldn't expect to find them is a little like doing a traffic survey in your driveway instead of on the interstate," charges Erik Olson of the National Wildlife Federation.[7] One of the most common pesticides found in groundwater is aldicarb—the most acutely toxic pesticide still used today. Among other places, aldicarb has been found in the groundwater of Long Island, the only drinking water source for 3 million people.

Some pesticides can persist for very long times in the environment, and make their way up the food chain. Nearly all Americans have residues of the pesticides DDT, chlordane, heptachlor, aldrin, and dieldrin in their bodies, even though all of these chemicals were banned from agricultural use between 1972 and 1982. DDT has been found in animals in the Antarctic and other areas where it was never used. Large numbers of honey bees and wild bees are poisoned by pesticides. The resulting honey losses and reduction in crop pollination costs some $150 million annually. In addition, pesticide use causes at least $15 million in fishery and wildlife losses every year.[8]

Pesticide resistance. Meanwhile, more and more pests are developing resistance to pesticides. According to the National Academy of Sciences (NAS), before World War II only 7 species of insects and mites were known to be resistant to the few chemical insecticides in use then. By 1984, at least 447 species were resistant to one or more insecticides. In 1986, the NAS noted that there were no longer any effective chemical insecticides for controlling some major crop pests in some areas, including the

---

Fruit and vegetable superstars

Nutrition-wise, it's hard to go wrong with fresh fruits and vegetables. Except for avocados, they're all low in fat and most are packed with fiber, vitamins, and minerals, especially vitamins A and C. But there are some real superstars in the produce department—because of their high fiber and/or vitamin content, you'd do well to make them regulars in your diet. Here are some of the very best:

➤ **Vegetables:** spinach, collard greens, and kale; sweet potato or potato (baked, with the skin); acorn or butternut squash; and broccoli and asparagus.

➤ **Fruits:** watermelon, papaya, cantaloupe, mango, orange, grapefruit, banana, honeydew melon, and strawberries.

Keep in mind that fresh or frozen food always beats canned. Canned vegetables are high in salt and canned fruit usually has added sugar and less vitamin C and fiber. Vegetables usually taste best and are most nutritious if they're steamed or cooked only lightly. And fruits are a good source of fiber, while fruit juices have very little. Go easy on dried fruits—their natural sugars are sticky and can promote tooth decay.

Colorado potato beetle in Long Island.[9] Today, although farmers are using more than 30 times more pesticides than in 1945, the portion of the harvest lost to pests has increased by 20 percent.[10]

Pesticides in food. Some 350 active pesticide ingredients are allowed for use on food crops—at least 70 of which have been classified by the EPA as probable or possible human carcinogens.[11] To be honest, no one knows for sure how many cancers are caused by exposure to pesticides in food. (Tumors don't come with signs saying, "I'm from the captan on the spinach you've been eating since 1960.") A 1987 National Academy of Sciences report highlighted some of the problems related to pesticides.[12] Also in 1987, the EPA ranked pesticide residues in food third in terms of cancer risk, of 31 problems under their jurisdiction.[13]

Risks to farmers and farm workers. Even if it's hard to prove a direct cause-and-effect link between eating pesticide residues in food and getting cancer, mounting evidence indicates that occupational exposures to pesticides increase farmers' and farm workers' risks of cancer and other acute illnesses. The National Cancer Institute (NCI) found, for instance, that the herbicide 2,4-D was associated with a three fold increase in the risk of non-Hodgkins lymphoma in Nebraska farmers[14] and a six fold increase in Kansas farmers[15] exposed for more than 20 days per year. NCI also found that flour-mill employees, who frequently use pesticides to fumigate the flour, also were at increased risk for developing non-Hodgkins lymphoma.[16]

A particularly serious concern is with pesticides that are neurotoxic, or nerve-damaging. Canadian researchers found that the major agricultural region in Quebec had almost six times the rate of Parkinson's disease as the areas in the province with the least pesticide use.[17] According to the congressional Office of Technology Assessment, the most neurotoxic classes of pesticides (organophosphorus and carbamate insecticides) pose "a significant threat to a substantial portion of the 4 to 5 million Americans who work in agriculture."[18]

The United Farm Workers (UFW), led by Cesar Chavez, has worked for two decades to publicize the serious occupational hazards faced by farmers and farm workers. According to the UFW, pesticides are responsible for cancer, behavioral changes, birth defects, and miscarriages among farmers, farm workers, and their families. The UFW has called for a boycott of fresh table grapes grown in California until grape growers stop using five pesticides most dangerous to workers (captan, parathion, phosdrin, methyl bromide, and dinoseb). Of these, dinoseb has been banned, and the EPA was considering recommendations to ban parathion as this book went to press. Chavez makes an important point that consumers who are concerned about the small amounts of pesticides on their fruit and vegetables should also be concerned about the farm workers and their families who breathe in and ingest much greater amounts of these poisons.

FARM-FRESH, ORGANICALLY GROWN

Because of all these problems, it isn't surprising that everywhere from farms to supermarket chains, there is new interest in organic food, and in the agricultural methods that produce it. While the goal of conventional agriculture is to maximize production, the goal of "sustainable" agriculture—which includes organic farming —is to ensure the long-term sustainability of production. Sustainable agriculture emphasizes conservation of soil, water, energy, and biological resources; protection of wildlife and biological diversity; reduction of the use of synthetic chemicals (and ultimately fewer synthetic residues on food); and better health of farmers and farm workers—all while ensuring profits for farmers and rural communities.

Organic farming was derided for many years by the agricultural establishment, but that scorn was often a result of the fear of losing profits from the sale of chemicals rather than looking at the facts. A landmark 1980 report published by the USDA rebutted the then-fashionable charge that switching to organic farming methods would lead to mass starvation. Instead, the researchers found that "a large number of farmers who operate small farms could change to organic farming with little economic impact on the U.S. economy." After looking at some of the benefits of organic farming, the researchers concluded the report by saying, "the team feels strongly that research and education programs should be developed to address the needs and problems of organic farmers."[19]

Rave review for organic food

When you buy organic food, you're not just minimizing your own exposure to pesticide residues—you're also getting food that was raised without damaging the environment or threatening farmers' and farm workers' health. Organic aficionados also like to point out how simply delicious organic food can be.

In 1987, Marion Burros, a food columnist for *The New York Times*, sampled organic food from 12 mail-order suppliers, and raved about the taste. Organic navel oranges from one California supplier were "superbly sweet," she said. The organically grown prunes she sampled were "the biggest, fattest and sweetest ever tasted."

Organic chicken from New York was "extraordinary—white in color, with very little fat and very flavorful." A Canadian brand of organic 15-grain cereal was "outstanding." And organic produce from a Pennsylvania supplier was "exceptional, especially the broccoli, beets, and winter squashes. All were full of flavor and delicious served without seasoning."

Shortly after the report was published, the incoming Reagan administration closed the USDA office that sponsored the report and fired the person who coordinated the study team's work. It wasn't until 1990, and many pesticide scares later, that Congress passed a law requiring a standard definition of "organic," and progress at the national level toward organic farming resumed.

Meanwhile, organic food was catching on in the marketplace. In 1980 sales of organic food totaled $174 million; by 1988 the industry was valued at $893 million, and in 1989, $1.25 billion. In 1990 suppliers of certified organic produce represented just 3 percent of the produce market, but some experts predict that figure will increase to 9 percent by 1995.[20]

Short of switching entirely to organic farming, farmers have many ways to reduce their reliance on pesticides. One way is through a practice called Integrated Pest Management (IPM). IPM involves a range of methods, such as planting a crop a little earlier to beat the bugs, using a pest-resistant variety, or spraying only when pests have reached a level that will cause economic damage to a crop. Another way to reduce pesticide use is to discourage pests naturally through crop rotation. According to Cornell's David Pimentel, during the early 1940s, little or no insecticide was applied to corn, and losses to insects were only 3.5 percent. Since then, insecticide use on corn has grown more than 1,000-fold, but losses due to insects have increased to 12 percent—primarily because of the abandonment of crop rotations.[21]

Other countries already have programs under way for significantly reducing pesticide use. In 1985, Denmark developed a plan for reducing pesticide use there by 50 percent by 1997. Sweden adopted a program in 1988 for reducing pesticide use by 50 percent within 5 years. And the Netherlands is also developing a program for cutting pesticide use in half within 10 years.

It's possible in the United States as well. In fact, Pimentel has estimated that if pesticide use here were reduced by one half while using other methods to maintain crop yields, the total price increase to consumers would be only 0.6 percent. That's not much of a price for protecting the environment and human health. As one supermarket executive puts it, "We're not looking at something that's going to happen overnight, but within ten years I can see a great reduction in pesticide residues—if the consumer asks for it."[22]

THE REGULATORY SHORTCOMINGS

Meanwhile, it's up to the government to keep the food supply safe. But government regulation of pesticides in produce and grains falls short in a number of ways.

The EPA is required to set safe maximum legal limits—called "tolerances"—for pesticide residues in food. But the EPA's starting point in setting tolerances isn't safety—instead, it's the amount of pesticide left after being applied at a rate recommended by the manufacturer. The EPA is then required to "balance" the

---

Organic success story

Leland Eickerman, a farmer in Bourbon, Missouri, had fallen on hard times financially. Like many other farmers, he was growing the conventional crops, the conventional way—producing corn and soybeans on large tracts of land, and routinely spraying them with pesticides.

Finally, Leland decided to make a big switch: he let go of a lot of the land he had been renting, and kept a small tract where he grew vegetables.

Today he farms livestock and a wide variety of organic vegetables that he markets himself, directly to consumers and farmers markets. His profits? Better than ever.

What does "organic" mean?

Ripe, red tomatoes at the farmers' market...corn meal at the local food co-op...bags of crisp carrots at the supermarket—all of them labeled "organically grown." Sales of organic food have quadrupled over the past decade. But until recently, there haven't been uniform, national standards to define what "organic" really means. Instead, half of the states have had their own standards, with varying levels of stringency, for organic food production. And some foods labeled organic may not have been grown organically at all.

But that is all about to change. New federal legislation—the Food, Agriculture, Conservation and Trade Act of 1990 (the 1990 "Farm Bill")—requires the first-ever national standards for producing organic foods, and a mandatory certification program, to be administered by the states, with third-party certifying agents to be accredited by the USDA, to ensure compliance with the standards. Under the law, which should be implemented in late 1993:

➤ National standards will be developed by a national organic standards board for growing and processing all organic food. The standards will require that organic food be grown without the use of most synthetic fertilizers or pesticides (with extremely limited exceptions, which must be approved by the organic standards board).

➤ Standards will be developed for the first time for certified organic meat, milk, and eggs. Although some states have had livestock and poultry standards, none of them has been fully developed and implemented because the USDA has actually prohibited the labeling and sale of meat as organic.

➤ Organic farmers, food handlers, and food processors will be required to maintain extensive records to demonstrate their compliance with the organic production standards, and farms will be subject to unannounced inspections, residue tests, and soil testing.

➤ Food produced according to the organic standards will have state-approved "organically grown" labels identifying the certifying agent.

benefits of the pesticide with the risks. But for many of the tolerances now in effect the EPA's balancing act relied on inadequate safety data. In 1982, a Congressional committee concluded that the cancer data was inadequate for about four-fifths of the 1,200 registered and commercially used pesticides, and that data on the ability of pesticides to cause mutations was inadequate for more than 90 percent of them.[23]

In 1972, the EPA was directed by Congress to begin re-evaluating the use of previously registered pesticides according to current safety data requirements and scientific standards. Having made no progress, the EPA was again mandated by Congress in 1988 to complete its re-evaluation by 1997. But the task is monumental—most of the 300 pesticides used on food have to be reregistered. As of January 1991, the EPA had completely re-evaluated just two of them.[24] Meanwhile, the pesticides remain on the market and in use on food.

The current tolerances for most pesticides are based on outdated estimates of how much produce Americans eat. When these tolerances were set, the government assumed, for instance, that the average American ate no more than half a cantaloupe a year, one and a half cups of cooked summer squash, and two and a half tangerines. If you happen to eat more than this "average," you could be exposed to a level of risk above what the government says is safe. The EPA is now using more up-to-date dietary information, and all pesticides will eventually be re-evaluated using the more realistic assumptions. But until the re-evaluation is complete, which will take years, the old tolerances remain in effect.

The EPA isn't the only federal agency at fault. The FDA is responsible for monitoring food for pesticide residues and enforcing the limits set by the EPA. But the FDA spot-checks only a tiny fraction—less than 1 percent—of food shipments for illegal pesticide residues.[25]

What's more, the FDA doesn't even test regularly for a large number of pesticides that may be present in food. The FDA has developed five "multi-residue" testing methods that together can detect fewer than half of the pesticide residues that might be in food. It doesn't regularly test for pesticides that aren't detected by these multiresidue methods—including 33 pesticides that the FDA itself classifies as posing a "moderate to high" health hazard.[26] And even when the FDA does detect illegal pesticide residues on food, the laboratory tests usually aren't available in time to stop the contaminated food from being sold and eaten.

For imported produce, the situation isn't any better. In 1986 the General Accounting Office (GAO), the investigative arm of Congress, reported that the FDA samples less than 1 percent of the million or so imported food shipments a year. Between 1979 and 1985, the FDA found that 6 percent of the imported food samples it analyzed contained illegal pesticide residues. Seventy-three out of 164 adulterated samples were not recovered "and are presumed to have been consumed by the public."[27] At a 1987 congressional hearing, FDA officials acknowledged that not a single pineapple imported from the Philippines had been inspected, even though the agency knew that the pineapples had been treated with heptachlor, a cancer-causing pesticide banned in the United States since 1978.

"Active" pesticide ingredients receive most of the regulatory attention, but they aren't the only cause for concern. Typically, the volume of active ingredients in a pesticide is exceeded by that of the "inert" ingredients, such as solvents, wetting and sticking agents, and preservatives. These inerts can be as harmful to humans as the active ingredients are, but they are often not tested for toxicity and are generally exempt from the residue tolerance requirements. (For example, dioxane is a so-called inert ingredient which is considered possibly carcinogenic to humans.) By 1989 the EPA had identified 40 of the approximately 1,200 inert ingredients contained in pesticide products as carcinogenic, neurotoxic, or "of toxicological concern." More than 800 inerts lack adequate data on toxicity.[28]

Under current law, pesticides generally cannot be banned just because they cause cancer. Thus, the EPA has set official tolerances that specify the amount of cancer-causing pesticides that can remain on fresh fruits and veg-

The great Alar scare

There was aminotriazole in cranberries, EDB in bread, and most recently—and probably most notoriously—Alar in apples.

Alar, the trade name for daminozide, had been used since 1968 to enhance the color and firmness of apples and to control the time it takes apples to ripen. Although most people hadn't heard of it until 1989, environmental groups had been fighting for years to have it banned because of concerns that it could increase people's risk of cancer. In 1989, the Natural Resources Defense Council (NRDC) published a report that highlighted the risks to children of 23 pesticides, including Alar.[29] Industry and government officials tried to reassure the public that hardly any growers were using Alar, and that apples and apple products didn't contain any residues of the chemical—claims that were quickly disproven in independent testing by Consumers Union.[30]

Many people reacted to the controversy by throwing apples and apple juice down the kitchen sink. Apple sales plummeted. Alar's manufacturer (Uniroyal) took the chemical off the market, although it vehemently defended Alar as being "perfectly safe," and warned that the loss of Alar would seriously affect apple yields (it didn't). Finally, five years after the EPA first acknowledged the cancer-causing potential of Alar, the EPA banned it. The apple industry was

etables. The one exception, through a fluke in the law, is for carcinogenic pesticides that occur in processed foods in amounts greater than are present in the raw commodity. For example, if tomatoes tainted with cancer-causing pesticides are converted into tomato paste, the EPA could prevent the tomato paste from being sold. It could, but it doesn't—the EPA generally has not enforced this narrow provision of the law for chemicals now in use. It has prevented some new cancer-causing pesticides from being registered, however.

incensed over lost sales, and some growers even sued NRDC and CBS, whose "60 Minutes" program first broke the news about Alar.

In fact, the EPA's estimate of risk didn't differ that much from the NRDC's. But the data can be viewed in different ways. According to EPA estimates, if Alar remained in use, it could have caused nearly 11,000 additional cancer deaths by the year 2033. That sounds pretty outrageous, and it is. But using the same EPA estimate, Alar increased an individual's risk of dying of cancer by 5 thousandths of 1 percent. That risk pales next to the risks from smoking, eating a high-fat diet, or consuming too much alcohol. In other words, the same risk that could result in thousands of deaths in the population at large poses a pretty small danger to one person.

The lesson for consumers is to not over react to headlines—and to insist on government protection of the food supply. The lesson to industries using dangerous pesticides is to act responsibly and take action early to reduce risks and avert a crisis. Alar, like dozens of other chemicals in our food and environment, deserved to be eliminated because it posed an unacceptably large risk to society. It should have been banned years ago. But it wasn't worth panicking over.

Industry and public-interest groups in Washington are battling over whether that section of the law, a sword hanging over the food-processing industry's head, should be repealed. A committee of the National Academy of Sciences, the EPA, the FDA, Congressman Henry Waxman (the chairman of the House Subcommittee on Health and the Environment), and a few environmental organizations have supported changing the law to permit processed foods to contain a pesticide that is estimated to pose a "negligible" risk of cancer. But they would extend that negligible-risk rule to all pesticide uses, on both fresh and processed foods.

Such a law would replace the current system that allows government regulators to balance economic benefits to farmers, distributors, and processors against health risks to consumers. Currently if chemical X is highly effective at preventing mold growth, it might be permitted even if it theoretically could cause dozens of cancer deaths a year. Some environmental groups, though, urge that cancer-causing pesticides never be allowed, because there is no scientifically defensible way to determine safe levels for carcinogens. And, particularly if safer substitutes are available, it only makes sense to stop using carcinogenic pesticides.

WHO'S PROTECTING THE CHILDREN?

The regulatory failings are especially serious when it comes to protecting children, who may be even more vulnerable to pesticides than adults are. For one thing, children eat more produce, relative to their size and weight, than adults do. Preschoolers, for instance, consume six times as much fruit, which means that children are exposed to higher levels of pesticides. In estimating exposure to eight carcinogenic pesticides, the Natural Resources Defense Council (NRDC) found that preschoolers received four times greater exposure, on average, than adults did. But since the EPA rarely takes children's eating patterns into account when it sets tolerances, it may underestimate children's exposure to pesticides in food. For the parent trying to feed a child a safe, healthy diet, that's not very reassuring.

Another problem is that children may be more susceptible to pesticides' toxic effects. This is particularly problematic for carcinogenic pesticides, since cancer could be initiated more readily during the periods of rapid cell division occurring in infancy and early childhood. What's more, children have the rest of their lives ahead of them, and thus more time for cancer to develop. It's one thing if you're 65 years old when you are first exposed to a carcinogen that takes, say, 25 years to manifest itself; it's something else if you are exposed to that carcinogen beginning at age three.

THAT PERFECT PEACH ...
THAT WAXY SHINE

Someone offers you a choice between two tomatoes: one is red and flawless, and the other is greenish-orange and misshapen. Which do you pick? Probably the perfect red one. And that's part of the problem.

Pesticides are often used to prevent blemishes, in order to make food look more appealing to consumers. Of course, great looks don't guarantee great taste, as anyone knows who has eaten a "perfect" but tasteless store-bought tomato. That funny-looking misshapen tomato might taste better and have a lot less pesticide residue on it.

According to the National Academy of Sciences, many fruits and vegetables have to meet government or industry standards that set a premium on good looks and other qualities that have little to do with taste, safety, or nutritional value.[31] Farmers are practically forced to overuse pesticides in order to meet these standards:

➤ Farmers choose tomato strains that are disease resistant, have tough skins, and a slightly square shape for better packing, and douse them with pesticides to "make the grade."

➤ About two-thirds of the pesticides used on California tomatoes grown for processing (for example, into tomato sauce) are used in order to meet cosmetic standards that limit damage by the tomato fruit worm.[32] But tomatoes that are processed are crushed, so the damage would never even be visible.

➤ Peaches receive intensive pesticide applications to keep them looking pretty, among other reasons, according to Lawrie Mott, a senior scientist with the Natural Resources Defense Council. "More than half the peaches tested between 1982 and 1985 by federal and California monitoring programs contained pesticide residues," she notes.

➤ Perfect-looking oranges command twice the price of oranges that have thrip scars (which only affect the rind, not the fruit). According to University of California, Riverside, professor Joseph Morse, Ph.D., more than 33 percent of all insecticides sprayed on California oranges—over 400,000 pounds—are used to control thrips. Parathion and dimethoate, two very toxic pesticides, are commonly used.[33]

The practice of coating fruits and vegetables with wax to make them look good and increase their marketability is also a potential problem. These waxes—which are used to replace the natural waxes that are

Organic for baby

If you're concerned about pesticides in your child's food, and especially if your child tends to eat a lot of one particular fruit or vegetable, consider buying certified organically grown food.

Earth's Best, a Vermont-based company, makes certified organic baby food that is available in about 3,000 supermarkets and in many health-food stores. And a new line of certified organic baby food, "Beech-Nut's Special Harvest," should eventually be available nationwide.

often lost during post-harvest washing—help prevent moisture loss and reduce shriveling and wilting of produce. The FDA has approved several waxes for use on produce, including shellac, beeswax, and carnauba wax. Although the FDA maintains that the waxes used on produce are safe, in some cases there isn't much safety data on them.

But even if the waxes themselves aren't a health hazard, the fungicides that are mixed with or covered up by the waxes may be. Fungicides are applied to retard spoilage during shipping and storage. The EPA has approved about a dozen fungicides for use post-harvest or in conjunction with wax. Of them, captan and folpet are listed by EPA as probable human carcinogens, and benomyl is listed as a possible human carcinogen. Unfortunately, waxes can seal pesticides into food, and they can't be washed off.

You often can't tell if produce has been waxed just by looking at it. And it's not just on waxy-looking produce such as cucumbers, apples, and bell peppers, either. In fact, peaches, sweet potatoes, tomatoes, squashes, eggplants, parsnips, turnips, and rutabagas may all be coated with waxes. A 50-year-old federal law[34] requires retailers to label produce that has been waxed, but the FDA relies on states to enforce this, and the states rarely do. The law doesn't require the disclosure of any pesticides used. One exception is the state of Maine, which has a "truth in labeling" law that requires stores to post information indicating that produce in the store has been treated after harvest, to label waxed produce, and to provide information about the specific pesticides and waxes used on produce sold in the store to any customer who requests it. That's just the kind of information we should all have in order to make educated choices.

Hold the aflatoxin

Aflatoxins are naturally occurring toxins produced by a type of mold that grows on grains and peanuts. Aflatoxins were identified in 1960 when more than 100,000 turkeys in the British Isles died from eating moldy peanut meal. Later testing showed aflatoxin to be a potent liver carcinogen in animal studies.

The hazards to humans aren't quite as clear. The International Agency for Research on Cancer (IARC) has classified aflatoxins among the 50 known human carcinogens. But a recent large epidemiological study conducted in China concluded that aflatoxins weren't associated with liver cancer in humans.[35]

Although the study casts some doubt on IARC's classification of aflatoxins, further research is needed before the cancer link can be dismissed. The industry and government should continue to take precautions to keep aflatoxin levels in food (and animal feed) as low as possible. Peanut growers and processors of peanut butter, for instance, follow voluntary "good manufacturing practices" that include monitoring for mold growth and testing samples for aflatoxins. But according to recent *Consumer Reports* testing,[36] small amounts of aflatoxins still make their way into peanut butter. Aflatoxins can also be found in moldy nuts and sprouted grains.

Safe Food choices

◆ You can probably play it safest by sticking to the large, national brands of peanut butter, which are apt to have the best quality control, and which contained the lowest aflatoxin levels in *Consumer Reports*' testing in 1990.

◆ Popcorn and sweet corn tend to resist mold and be free of aflatoxins. But aflatoxins can be found in peanuts, pecans, walnuts, almonds, Brazil nuts, and pistachios. When you shell or eat nuts, look at each one carefully, and throw out any that are moldy, discolored, or shriveled. If you bite into a nut that tastes bad, spit it out. And if you find mold on sprouted grains that you purchase or sprout yourself, throw them out.

CARCINOGENS AU NATUREL?

Forget synthetic pesticides for a minute. What about the "natural" pesticides in our fruit and vegetables? It appears that many plants contain substances that repel and poison pests. Should you be worrying more about these pesticides that Mother Nature has created than about the chemicals concocted in pesticide manufacturers' laboratories?

Bruce Ames, Ph.D., a professor of biochemistry and molecular biology at the University of California at Berkeley, has argued that the amount of synthetic pesticides in our food is insignificant compared to the natural pesticides that the plants themselves produce to defend against fungi, insects, and other predators. The pesticides in our diet, he claims, are "99.99 percent all natural." Moreover, he maintains that neither the natural nor the synthetic pesticides in our food pose a significant problem. Let's take a closer look at some of his arguments.

Ames claims that there are tens of thousands of "nature's pesticides," and that of those tested, about half are carcinogenic. The fact is, however, only 52 natural pesticides actually have been tested. And they are not necessarily representative of the others; in fact, they were probably tested precisely because they were suspected of being carcinogenic. Of these 52 chemicals, Ames says that 27 are carcinogenic, but even that is probably an overstatement.

Together, the U.S. National Toxicology Program and the International Agency for Research on Cancer (IARC) of the World Health Organization evaluated the evidence for 14 of Ames' 27 "natural carcinogens." There was good evidence that 6 of those 14 caused cancer in animals. The remaining 8 either had limited, inadequate, or inconsistent evidence of cancer. That's hardly "overwhelming" evidence of natural carcinogens in our diet.

63

What's in that cereal or loaf of bread?

Most of the exotic-sounding chemicals added to cereals and bread are actually quite safe—in fact, many of them are nutritious. Most cereals today are heavily fortified with vitamins and minerals, in part to replace nutrients lost in processing and to distract attention from the sugar content, which may be as high as 60 percent. Don't worry about such additives as thiamin mononitrate (vitamin B1), riboflavin (vitamin B2), and pyridoxine hydrochloride (vitamin B6). Calcium propionate is added to most commercial breads to prevent mold growth—not only is it not dangerous, but the calcium is a nutritious bonus. The mono- and diglycerides added to bread are safe substances that make for a softer loaf (if that's what you want). We discuss certain other additives in Chapter 7. Two grain-product ingredients, one rarely used and one common, do merit concern:

➤ **Psyllium** is a soluble fiber (actually obtained from a cultivated weed, grown mostly in India) that is used in some laxatives and as an additive in Kellogg's Heartwise cereal. Psyllium has been shown to lower blood cholesterol levels, and if cereal and bread manufacturers get the go-ahead from the FDA, they may start using it widely as an additive in their products. But before you rush out to get your daily dose, be aware that too much psyllium can cause bloating, gas, or diarrhea. In addition, a few people have experienced allergic reactions ranging from mild to life-threatening after eating psyllium in cereal. Apparently, those most at risk are nurses and others who are exposed to psyllium on the job—for instance, by mixing laxatives for patients and breathing psyllium fibers—and have developed a sensitivity to it. CSPI has recommended that the FDA require warning labels about allergic reactions on all food products containing psyllium, similar to the one on the laxative Metamucil. But in case the FDA doesn't follow CSPI's advice, watch out for psyllium on ingredient labels if you think you may be allergic to it.

▶ **Potassium bromate,** an additive in flour that improves the texture and volume of bread, has caused cancer in laboratory animals and is classified as a possible human carcinogen. Most potassium bromate breaks down into relatively harmless potassium bromide during baking. But in 1990, after British scientists discovered tiny amounts of potassium bromate in bread in retail stores, the British government banned the use of the additive in flour. American bakers say that all the potassium bromate turns into potassium bromide when bread is baked. For its part, the FDA has simply said that its detection methods aren't as sensitive as those used by the British scientists. Although the risk isn't high enough to recommend avoiding products containing potassium bromate, the FDA needs to improve its detection methods and conduct studies to ensure that the levels that are present in our food are really safe.

Ames has also argued that if we breed pest-resistant plants to reduce the use of synthetic pesticides, we will likely be breeding plants that have higher levels of natural toxins. He points to two examples: a new variety of insect-resistant celery that was found to have eight times the amount of toxic psoralens as normal celery, and a new type of potato that had to be withdrawn from the market because of increased levels of two natural toxins.

But in fact, there doesn't have to be a trade-off between synthetic and natural toxins. New crop varieties can be tested for their toxicity before they are widely released. And to rely solely on breeding to resist pests would be unwise anyway. Farmers can reduce synthetic pesticide use in a number of other ways.

Further, Ames and others have argued that many chemicals—natural or synthetic—that cause cancer in laboratory animals are not true carcinogens. The argument goes like this: The apparent carcinogenicity of many chemicals results from feeding them to animals at extremely high doses. The high dosages injure various tissues, and cancers result. None of that would happen if only small amounts of chemicals had been used in the tests.

But other scientists dispute every part of that argument. David Rall, M.D., Ph.D., former director of the National Toxicology Program, notes that about 90 percent of the chemicals studied that cause cancer at high dosages also cause cancer in animals at somewhat lower dosages.[37] Vincent James Cogliano, Ph.D., and his colleagues at the EPA have pointed out that tissue damage is probably the cause of at most a small fraction of cancers observed in laboratory animals.[38] Bernard Weinstein, M.D., of Columbia University's College of Physicians and Surgeons, argues that not only have almost all of the known human carcinogens tested positive in animals, but some compounds that caused cancer in animals later turned out to be human carcinogens.[39]

This argument won't be settled for a long time. "The fact is, I don't know what goes on at those low doses. Dr. Ames doesn't. Nobody does," says professor John C. Bailar.[40] But considering the terrible burden of cancer, an ugly and potentially fatal disease, isn't it better to be safe than sorry, and minimize our exposure to synthetic pesticides and other toxins?

Which isn't to say that consumers and regulators should ignore natural toxins. We should be testing them more, and taking steps to reduce both the natural and synthetic hazards in our food. The fact that there are naturally occurring toxins in food is certainly no excuse to add synthetic ones deliberately. As Edward Groth III, Ph.D., a scientist with Consumers Union, has put it, "Nature may not be benign, but She's blameless. She's not making a business decision to sell or spray chemicals, while someone else bears the risk."

SAFE FOOD CHOICES

Eat plenty of fresh fruits and vegetables and whole grains. Try for variety, too—that way you'll be assured of getting the full range of nutrients that different vegetables, fruits, and grains offer, and you will minimize your exposure to any one harmful contaminant.

AT THE MARKET

◆ Whenever possible, buy locally grown produce directly from farmers. It is almost always fresher than produce available in stores, and is picked closer to the peak of its ripeness. Even if it isn't grown organically, produce at farmers' markets and roadside stands isn't likely to have been waxed or sprayed with post-harvest pesticides because it is sold so soon after harvest and close to where it was grown. (But be warned: occasionally produce sold at farmers' markets and roadside stands is bought at wholesale markets and has been waxed and shipped long distances.) Fortunately, shopping at farmers' markets is an option for more and more people these days: the number of these markets around the country almost doubled from 1980 to 1990.[41] Shopping at farmers' markets has the added benefit of helping support small, family farms and organic farmers. It also gives you the chance to talk to farmers directly about how they grow food and to try varieties that may not be available at the grocery store. And because there are no intermediaries and transportation costs are low, prices may be lower than at supermarkets.

◆ Buy certified organic produce if you can—it is grown without synthetic chemical fertilizers or pesticides, and doesn't contain post-harvest fungicides. Certified organic food is often available in natural foods stores, food cooperatives, farmers' markets, or by mail (see page 214).

◆ When you can, buy domestically grown produce, and produce that is in season. Out-of-season produce is likely to be imported, and may contain pesticides that are banned in the United States. (Ironically, some pesticides that are banned in the United States are still produced here for export, and can turn up on imported produce.) Testing consistently turns up pesticide residues more often in imported than domestically grown bell peppers, broccoli, cantaloupe, cucumbers, green beans, grapes, and tomatoes. Be sure to look for domestically grown canned produce as well, such as canned tomatoes and tomato sauce—the labels should say if they're imported.

◆ When selecting fresh produce, don't shy away from less-than-perfect-looking fruits and vegetables. Perfect-looking produce may be that way because of excessive pesticide use (which makes it less than perfect safety-wise). Don't buy spoiled produce, of course—and avoid anything that is moldy—but you needn't worry about produce that is slightly discolored or misshapen.

Peeling and washing produce

To peel or not to peel? It's a toss-up: peeling does completely remove surface pesticides (whereas washing might not remove them all), but peeling can also mean losing valuable fiber and nutrients. As a general rule, peel produce if your diet is otherwise rich in fiber—especially produce that is obviously waxed, to remove the wax and any pesticides that might have been applied with it.

Always wash produce. Adding a few drops of dish soap to a pint of water is more effective than plain water at removing many pesticides. Just choose a soap brand that isn't loaded with dyes and perfumes. Don't use salt water or vinegar—they won't help, and salt is something we get more than enough of anyway. And there's no evidence that those specially formulated pesticide- and wax-removing washes are more effective than regular dish detergent—and they cost up to 8 times as much. Use a vegetable brush, and be sure to rinse completely.

Here are some tips for handling specific types of produce (short of buying organic food):

◆ For leafy vegetables like lettuce and cabbage, discard the outer leaves and wash the inner leaves.

◆ Wash celery after trimming off the leaves and tops.

◆ For recipes that call for grated peel, buy organic fruit if possible.

◆ Peel carrots (you won't be losing out on fiber, since it is found throughout). Peel cucumbers if they're waxed. Peel apples, peaches, and pears if you get plenty of fiber from other sources, since these are most apt to contain risky residues.

◆ Wash eggplants, peppers, tomatoes, potatoes, green beans, cherries, grapes, and strawberries. Cut or chop up cauliflower, broccoli, and spinach before you wash them, since pesticides may be hard to wash off otherwise.

High-tech solutions? Biotechnology

The basic molecular-biology research of the 1960s and 1970s has paved the way for applied research and all sorts of new products. Biotechnology essentially means altering life forms and generating natural chemicals found in living organisms through the use of gene-splicing and other methods.

Many of the most interesting developments of biotechnology are occurring in agriculture and food technology. In labs across the country:

➤ Scientists have genetically engineered carrots with 25 percent more beta-carotene than normal, and are hoping for the day when they can produce foods with specifically enhanced nutritional qualities—more soluble fiber, say, or more calcium.

➤ Potatoes and alfalfa have been engineered to resist certain pests. Tomatoes have been developed that can be picked when red and ripe, and stay firm for three weeks.

➤ Livestock specialists have crossed a goat with a sheep, dubbing the offspring a "geep."

➤ Biotechnologists are attempting to develop rice and other crops that could "fix" nitrogen (something that only legume crops do naturally). If it works, this could greatly reduce the need for costly, polluting synthetic nitrogen fertilizers.

It all sounds promising—and it is—but biotechnology needs to be properly directed and controlled if it's really going to benefit the public, instead of just creating new corporate profits. For all the promising new developments in biotechnology, there are plenty of concerns, too. For instance, there's the much-touted potential of biotechnology to reduce our reliance on pesticides by developing pest-resistant crops. But these crops will need to be tested to make sure that we're not trading off the risks of synthetic pesticides for natural toxins.

A more serious concern is that biotechnology could further entrench pesticide use. In fact, major efforts are under way to create plant strains that are resistant not to pests, but to the harmful effects of herbicides, so that the herbicides can be used on a broader variety of crops. A concern is that once these genetically-engineered crops are in widespread use, not only might more herbicides be used, but herbicide-tolerant genes could spread, and ultimately result in the need to develop and use more herbicides to control herbicide-resistant weeds.

Similarly, biotechnology could improve animal production by creating breeds that are leaner or more resistant to disease, or by genetically engineering better vaccines to prevent animal disease. But it could also be used to increase the output of food animals, and thus add to animal stress and disease, which is a concern with the genetically engineered bovine growth hormone. (See page 83.)

What's needed is effective regulation to ensure that we choose biotechnologies that are ethical and that make good sense. At the least, regulatory agencies should require that proposed biotechnologies meet specified public-interest criteria, such as decreasing pollution or encouraging sustainable agriculture methods that eliminate or decrease the use of pesticides. In addition, regulators should require an assessment of overall costs and benefits to society before proposed biotechnology applications can be approved.

IN YOUR KITCHEN

◆ Wash fruits and vegetables thoroughly, and peel when appropriate. (See page 69 for specific tips on washing and peeling.) Washing can remove some, though not all, of the surface residues of pesticides; unfortunately, some pesticides are formulated to be insoluble to keep them from washing off crops when it rains. "Systemic" pesticide residues—those that are taken up by the plants and are thus inside the food—can't be removed either by washing or by peeling.

◆ Store potatoes in a cool, dark place. Trim away any green or damaged parts. That's because these parts may contain glycoalkaloids such as solanine—a natural toxin that affects the nervous system much the same way some pesticides, like malathion or parathion, do. Generally, breeders of potatoes monitor for alkaloid content. Solanine isn't destroyed when potatoes are cooked. It doesn't accumulate in the body, though.[42]

◆ Remember that produce (even organic produce) can carry disease-producing bacteria, including salmonella and listeria—another good reason to scrub fruit and vegetables carefully.

IN YOUR GARDEN

Nothing beats growing your own fruits and vegetables, whether it's one tomato plant on your patio or a large plot at a local community garden. Having a garden lets you control exactly what goes on and into your food…and might give you some appreciation of the extra savvy that organic farmers must use in place of pesticides. Gardening is an especially good way to introduce kids to the wonders of nature and the delicious tastes of truly fresh foods. Even kids who turn up their noses at anything green on their plates will find it hard not to enjoy their home-grown veggies. Here are some steps to successful organic gardening at home (see page 208 for more organic gardening resources):

◆ Plan ahead—plan to grow some lettuce, at least a row of beans, and tomatoes; don't plant too many root crops the first year, since your soil will probably need building before you can raise those successfully. Include plants such as marigolds, zinnias, cosmos, fennel, dill, daisies, and nasturtiums that help resist pests.

◆ Get seeds from mail-order catalogs (order them months ahead) or garden-supply stores, or buy plants that can be transplanted to your garden.

◆ Choose a sunny spot, with good drainage and easy access to a water hose.

◆ Start small—at most 20 by 20 feet.

◆ Prepare the soil by turning it over. Get it tested for pH, potassium, and phosphorus levels; your local extension service office or local nursery can usually do these tests for you (be sure to tell them you're gardening organically). Build the soil gradually with organic materials, including compost and organic fertilizer.

◆ Don't plant everything in tidy rows. Growing a diversity of crops and varying your planting arrangements can outsmart harmful insects. Change locations from year to year for each crop. Keep corn together for pollination, and don't plant tall crops where they'll keep the sun from reaching shorter crops.

◆ Water deeply once a week during dry weather. Conserve water by mulching.

◆ Use monthly applications of dilute fish emulsion or liquid seaweed on tomatoes and peppers.

◆ Check your garden every day and evening for pests, and pick them off by hand, or use traps.

Obstruct flying pests by using row covers, but remove them in time to allow pollination. In case of severe infestation, use insect soap if necessary (some gardeners recommend using diluted Ivory soap).

◆ Try importing helpful insects, such as lady bugs, to eat the plant-eating bugs. This is ecology in action!

◆ Rotate crops to disrupt insect and disease cycles, and at the end of the season remove weak and dying plants and debris to keep insects and disease from overwintering in your garden. The best defense against pests and disease is good overall plant health.

AS A CITIZEN

Rosalie Ziomek is a housewife and former psychotherapist in suburban Chicago whose concern about contaminated food spurred her to create Illinois Consumers for Safe Food. With just a couple of her friends—and endless energy—she persuaded two Chicago-area grocery chains, Jewel Food Stores and Dominick's Finer Foods, to disclose to customers the presence of wax on produce. She also helped convince Sunset Foods to disclose the presence of post-harvest pesticides. Inspired by her example? Here are some things you can do:

◆ If organically grown produce isn't available in your supermarket, ask the produce manager to stock it. Because of problems such as seasonal fluctuations in supply and the smaller volumes involved, it can be difficult for supermarkets to stock organic produce. But you should have the choice to buy organic food. If your supermarket seems to have legitimate problems in stocking fresh organic produce, ask them at least to offer packaged organic food, such as organically grown grains, juices, frozen food, or baby food.

◆ Ask your supermarket manager to comply with—and your state attorney general to enforce—the law and to label produce that has been waxed. Violators can be fined

$1,000 or be sent to prison for a year. Knowing that nonorganic produce is waxed alerts you to the possibility that it's been treated with post-harvest pesticides as well. Better still, work to get your supermarket to provide full labeling of produce, including its origin and information on any pesticides or waxes used on it. Ask your supermarket to refuse to stock produce treated with cancer-causing or dangerous neurotoxic chemicals.

◆ Write to food processors, produce distributors, and restaurant chains—and demand certified organic food. They listen to their customers!

◆ Buy a "share" in the harvest of an organic farm. Farming programs in communities across the country allow consumers to pay organic farmers in advance for a portion of the farmers' harvest. Share-owners typically collect their fresh food either from the farm or an urban distribution point once or twice a week during the growing season. These "community supported agriculture" programs benefit the consumers, who get a steady supply of fresh organic produce at reasonable rates, as well as the farmers, who are guaranteed a market for their production. (For help getting started, see page 208.)

◆ Write to your congressional representatives, and urge them to require a 50-percent reduction in pesticide use, and to phase out cancer-causing and other dangerous pesticides by the year 2000, and to improve monitoring for pesticide residues in food.

◆ Write to the USDA to urge it to promptly implement new standards for producing organic food, and to provide incentives that encourage farmers to use agricultural methods that rely on fewer or no pesticides.

◆ Urge universities to conduct research and training for farmers in sustainable agricultural methods that rely on fewer or no pesticides and synthetic fertilizers. Ask your governor and state legislators to promote sustainable agriculture.

CHAPTER 3

MILK & CHEESE

MILK & CHEESE

When you pour yourself and your child a tall glass of cold skim milk, you know you're treating yourselves to essential nutrients. Milk and other dairy products are a rich source of the calcium your body needs. (Women and adolescents in particular need plenty of calcium, which may help to prevent the bone disease osteoporosis.) Especially since milk is such an important staple in some children's diets, we have the right to expect it to be as safe and wholesome as the government and the dairy industry would have us believe it is.

So, isn't it? Maybe so, maybe not. There is a fair chance that the glass of milk you had with your lunch today—or the bottle of milk you fed your baby before nap time—contained traces of drugs given to dairy cows.

But that doesn't mean you should stop drinking milk or stop giving it to your children. The risks from any veterinary drugs that might be in the milk you buy aren't high enough for that. (The government certainly should be doing something, however—more on that later.) As for another possible problem with milk and milk products—bacterial contamination— you can do several things to keep the problem under control, including buying only pasteurized (never raw) milk and milk products, and taking precautions to prevent bacteria from proliferating.

A recent safety concern for pregnant women and people with weak immune systems, in particular, has been contamination of cheese by dangerous listeria bacteria. But since this problem has been associated mainly with certain kinds of soft cheeses, concerned individuals can minimize their risks by avoiding these products. As far as pesticides are concerned, the FDA rarely finds pesticide residues in milk and milk products.

WHAT'S THE MATTER WITH MILK?

Most of the milk that we drink today comes from cows confined on factory-like farms, where, as John Robbins describes it in *Diet for a New America,* the modern-day Bessie is "bred, fed, medicated, inseminated, and manipulated to a single purpose—maximum milk production at a minimum cost."[1] The average commercial dairy cow today is much larger and produces three or more times as much milk a year as cows used to produce. Whereas under natural conditions, a cow would live 10 to 15 years, in today's factory-like conditions, a cow may be culled out of a herd after only three or four years of production. During that shortened period of heavy production, the dairy cow is particularly prone to stress and disease. And farmers, who obviously want sick cows back "on line" producing milk as quickly as possible, have an arsenal of veterinary drugs at their disposal. The drugs—including drugs that are not approved for use on dairy cows—are widely available without prescription, even at farm feed stores.

When a dairy cow is given drugs, drug residues can go straight to the cow's milk. If a farmer fails (accidentally or deliberately) to observe a long enough "withdrawal" time, during which milk must be thrown away while drugs pass out of a cow's system, the drug-contaminated milk gets into the milk supply. The milk from just one cow given certain drugs can contaminate an entire tank-truck load with illegal drug residues, according to the FDA. For some drugs, approved withdrawal times have never been determined, so farmers or veterinarians using these drugs to treat dairy cows don't know how long milk may be contaminated.

Some drugs used in dairy cattle are capable, even at
low levels, of causing allergic reactions in a small fraction
of milk drinkers. Milk is the most common cause of food
allergy, and it's conceivable that in some cases the offending substance may not be the milk, but traces of drugs.
Some veterinary drugs (such as sulfamethazine and perhaps other sulfa drugs) may slightly increase cancer risks
for humans. What's more, the greater the use of antibiotic
drugs (including veterinary drugs), the more resistant bacteria become to them. If you are unlucky enough to
become infected with drug-resistant bacteria, the antibiotics your doctor prescribes may not help you get well.

The government has not done enough to protect the
public:

Inadequate testing. In spite of repeated assurances
by the government that the milk supply is safe, the
General Accounting Office has concluded that the FDA
doesn't really know if it is safe or not. Until recently, the

Healthy food choice: Dear dairy

Dairy products are high in saturated fat, so always choose the nonfat (skim) or low-fat varieties. With milk and yogurt that's easy—just
buy skim or 1-percent low-fat milk (2 percent isn't really low-fat),
low-fat buttermilk, and low-fat or nonfat yogurt. (Canned or dried
skim milk is fine—but canned condensed milk is high in fat and
added sugar.)

With cheese, lots of new products are available with fewer calories
and less fat. But making the right choice can still be difficult, since
terms like "light" or "part-skim" are vague. At least until tighter
FDA labeling regulations go into effect (see page 175), you'll have
to read the fine print on calorie and fat content. Try the new fat-free
frozen desserts, too—such as nonfat frozen yogurt, sorbet, Sealtest
Free, and Simple Pleasures. They are excellent substitutes for fatty
ice cream.

FDA itself did not routinely test milk for drug residues; instead it relied on the states to do their own testing—and didn't even regularly receive the states' testing results. (In February 1991, the FDA began a very limited program of testing five samples of milk a week for a handful of veterinary drugs—which is just a drop in the bucket.) What's more, the official testing method sanctioned by the FDA and used by most states to screen for drugs in milk—called the BS disc assay[2]—cannot even detect residues of most medications, other than penicillin-type antibiotics, that farmers use on lactating cows—legally or illegally.[3]

Misuse of veterinary drugs. In 1990, FDA officials reported that illegal veterinary drugs were found in 27 percent of 1,800 dairy barns checked.[4] What's more, the FDA itself allows unapproved veterinary drugs to be used on dairy cows. A congressional subcommittee revealed in 1990 that the FDA knows of at least 30 drugs not approved for use in dairy cows that are nonetheless used in milk-producing cows, 16 of them extensively, under the agency's "extra-label-use" policy.[5] This policy allows veterinary drugs to be used for purposes that have never been legally approved or proven safe. In 1985 Congress called the FDA's extra-label policy illegal, and recommended that it be halted, but the policy is still in effect.[6]

Tainted milk. Tests show that the milk supply does contain traces of veterinary drug residues. Between 1987 and 1989, four surveys by independent researchers found that between 63 and 86 percent of milk samples were tainted with sulfa drugs, tetracyclines, and other antibiotics.[7] In 1988, the FDA itself conducted a small survey of milk in 10 cities, and found traces of sulfamethazine (a suspected human carcinogen, illegal for use on dairy cows) in 74 percent of the samples. The agency and dairy industry responded with a "drug education" blitz for dairy farmers, and after further testing, the FDA announced that sulfamethazine use had been drastically reduced.

But in late 1989, testing done independently by both CSPI and *The Wall Street Journal* (using a more sensitive test than had been used in the previous surveys) together turned up low levels of animal drugs in milk in nearly one out of three samples. The drugs included sulfamethazine and other sulfa drugs, as well as penicillin, streptomycin, and erythromycin.[8] The FDA dismissed the results, saying that they might have been false positives, and again did its own testing. In February 1990 the FDA announced that its tests showed the milk supply contained no residues—but then, after congressional hearings, the FDA revealed that its testing had actually found small amounts of sulfa residues in almost 86 percent of the samples.[9] (And the veterinary drug problem goes well beyond milk. See page 97.)

All of this shouldn't stop you from drinking milk. But the fact is that our milk supply could and should be safer. Even if the risk from current levels of veterinary drug residues is small, it's an unnecessary risk. So the FDA should stop talking about how safe the milk supply is and instead do more to ensure that safety.

Much of the credit for disclosing the possible presence of veterinary drugs in milk belongs to Joseph Settepani, Ph.D., a career scientist in the veterinary medicine division of the FDA. Risking the fate that befalls many government whistle-blowers, Settepani helped educate journalists, legislators, and public-interest activists about drug contaminants after he tried, unsuccessfully, to persuade his supervisors to address the problem. His involvement was crucial to the public pressure that ultimately persuaded the FDA to improve its milk-testing policies. Dedicated government scientists like Settepani have played major roles over the years in providing the public with the unvarnished truth about many food additives, environmental contaminants, and workplace pollutants.

TINKERING WITH BESSIE'S HORMONES?

Depending on who you listen to, the U.S. milk supply may be the first major beneficiary, or the first victim, of another drug—this time a product of biotechnology.

At issue is bovine growth hormone (BGH), also called bovine somatotropin (BST), a hormone produced naturally in cows that stimulates milk production. Scientists have developed techniques for synthetically producing a BGH/BST that is almost identical to the natural hormone. When it's injected in dairy cows, BGH/BST can increase milk production by 10 to 25 percent. About 20,000 cows have already been treated experimentally with it, and since late 1985 the FDA has allowed milk from the BGH/BST-treated cows to be sold with the rest of the milk supply. The FDA is currently considering whether to allow the commercial use of the hormone, and may make its decision in 1992. But the intense controversy over BGH/BST isn't likely to die down, even if the hormone gets the government's go-ahead.[10]

Milk sensitivity

Even the purest milk is a problem for many people. An estimated 70 percent of the world's population—especially people of African and Asian descent—loses the enzyme needed to digest lactose, the naturally occurring sugar in milk. While most of these people don't experience any symptoms from drinking just one glass of milk at a time, up to one-third can get diarrhea, cramps, and other problems from that amount of milk or less.[11]

If you are so affected, you may be able to switch to yogurt, in which some of the lactose is digested by bacteria, or to dairy products with less lactose, such as cheese. Tablets that contain the enzyme can also be taken with or added to food to lower lactose levels. For more information on these tablets, call Dairy Ease 1-800-446-6267, Lactaid 1-800-257-8650, or Lactrase 1-800-558-5114.

Proponents of BGH/BST argue that it will lead to lower milk prices for consumers, without any harm to health. Opponents say that it won't affect milk prices, but that it will force many small dairy farmers out of business by increasing the milk supply in an already glutted market and driving down milk support prices to farmers. Opponents also question the safety of BGH/BST, both for humans and for animals. (The issue of animal health is also a human health issue, since more stressed and sick cows mean more veterinary drug use and a greater likelihood of drug residues in milk.)

In December 1990, an independent panel appointed by the National Institutes of Health concluded that BGH/BST was safe for humans. Its pronouncement on the question of animal health was more tentative. The panel said that the general health of dairy cows didn't seem to be "appreciably" affected, but it called for more research on the effects of BGH/BST on mastitis (a common inflammation of the udder that is a chief cause for the use of antibiotics in treating dairy cows).[12]

The panel also noted that it did not have access to unpublished data on BGH/BST—data the FDA claims it can't release until it makes its final decision on the hormone. (As this book went to press, the GAO and the Inspector General for the U.S. Department of Health and Human Services were investigating charges that the FDA and the corporate sponsors of BGH/BST have suppressed and manipulated data in efforts to get the hormone approved.)

The heated battle over BGH/BST raises basic questions that are part and parcel of modern life. First there's the age-old problem of technological threats to farmers. If it is approved, BGH/BST may very well push many farmers out of business—just as tractors, pesticides, and other developments did in the past. (Even without BGH/BST, for the past several decades about 100,000 farmers have been forced off the land each year.) Then, there's the public's skepticism of new technologies themselves. BGH/BST is a synthetic version of a natural substance. Could the small differences lead to human health risks, even if scientific studies don't detect any?

In light of the controversy over BGH/BST, the National Academy of Sciences should review the original scientific data on BGH/BST and provide the public with an objective evaluation of the health risks. Once the health question is resolved, we still face the other question: Is whatever benefit BGH/BST might offer more important than the survival of hundreds or thousands of family farms?

BATTLING BUGS IN MILK AND CHEESE

Another safety concern with dairy products is bacterial contamination—with the greatest risk posed by unpasteurized (raw) milk and raw-milk products. (The FDA has banned the interstate sale of raw milk.) Pasteurization kills most bacteria in milk, but pasteurized milk or milk products can also become contaminated. Pasteurization does not destroy nutrients. (For a detailed look at the problems of bacteria, see "Meet the bugs!" page 94.) Some of the largest outbreaks of food poisoning in the United States have been linked to milk or milk products:

➤ In 1982, an outbreak of food poisoning affecting some 17,000 people in Tennessee and nearby states was linked to pasteurized milk contaminated with *Yersinia enterocolitica* bacteria.

➤ In 1985, contaminated pasteurized milk from a Chicago dairy caused more than 16,000 confirmed (and as many as 200,000 unconfirmed) cases of salmonella food poisoning— several of them fatal—in six states. The salmonella was an antibiotic-resistant strain.

➤ In Southern California in 1985, 47 people died— the largest number of food-poisoning deaths recorded in recent U.S. history—after eating Mexican-style soft cheese contaminated with listeria—a rarer, but deadlier bacterium than salmonella. The cheese was made in part with raw milk; but an outbreak of listeriosis in Massachusetts in 1983 was linked to pasteurized milk.

The centralization of the food industry is partly to blame for large bacterial food poisoning outbreaks like these.[13] It used to be that when food-borne illness occurred, only people in the local area were affected, but today large plants market their products to millions of people. Changes in dairy processing may also contribute to the problem. For instance, most dairies now make several different products—including low-fat milk, skim milk, and chocolate milk—from the same pasteurized milk. When many processing steps take place after pasteurization, more opportunities arise for recontamination.

SAFE FOOD CHOICES

AT THE MARKET

◆ Buy only pasteurized milk and milk products.
◆ Pregnant women and people who are ill should avoid the kinds of cheese that have been frequently found to be contaminated with listeria. That means avoiding French Brie, Camembert, and Mexican-style soft cheese. (If you're healthy and not pregnant, the danger from listeria is minimal.)
◆ Buy organic cheese if you can—it's available in many stores that sell other organic foods.

Although currently it is nearly impossible to find organic milk in stores, tell your grocer you're interested in pasteurized organic milk. (Raw milk is not organic milk.) It should become more available as organic dairies become certified under the new federal organic labeling law (see "What does 'organic' mean?" page 53).

◆ Write to the Foundation on Economic Trends (see page 209) for a list of companies that have announced they will not knowingly accept dairy products from BGH/BST-treated cows. (Although the hormone hasn't been proven dangerous, it could lead to increased veterinary-drug use.) Then, if you're really committed, use your economic clout: If your favorite brand of dairy product isn't on the list, write to the company and ask them why not; and if your supermarket doesn't stock products from any of the companies listed, ask the manager to place an order.

IN YOUR KITCHEN

◆ Make sure your refrigerator maintains a temperature of 40 degrees F or colder, and keep milk refrigerated. Letting milk get warm for even two hours can allow bacterial growth and spoilage. If you like to have milk on your table for breakfast, pour a small amount into a serving pitcher. Don't pour leftover milk that has been standing at room temperature back into the original container, since it could contaminate the rest of the milk and cause it to spoil faster. Instead, cover the pitcher, re-refrigerate it, and then use it up quickly.

◆ Keep cheese refrigerated, too. Even though listeria can grow at low temperatures, it's still important to refrigerate food so that bacteria can't spread as quickly as they would if the food were left at room temperature.

◆ Use antibiotic drugs wisely. This may not seem like a food issue, but it could be. Antibiotics suppress the naturally occurring bacteria in your body, leaving you more vulnerable to disease-causing bacteria that may be resistant to antibiotics. So, when you're taking antibiotics, you are especially susceptible to infections from harmful bacteria in food. Take antibiotics only when they are appropriate; don't pressure your doctor to prescribe antibiotics for colds or other viral infections, since they're ineffective against these illnesses anyway. And if you have to take antibiotics, take them for as long as they are prescribed. Disease-causing bacteria can survive in your body even after the symptoms have disappeared. (Chapter 4 discusses antibiotic-resistant bacteria in greater detail.)

WHAT YOU CAN DO AS A CITIZEN

◆ Urge the FDA to do a better job of keeping drug residues out of the milk supply. Ask the agency to use tests that can detect low levels of a wide range of drug residues in milk, ban the use of cancer-causing veterinary drugs, phase out its extra-label-use policy, and require drug manufacturers to develop inexpensive and rapid screening tests for all the veterinary drugs they produce.

◆ Tell the FDA that you object to them allowing milk to be sold to unsuspecting consumers from cows treated with unapproved drugs, such as BGH/BST.

◆ Write the USDA to demand that it promptly implement new organic standards—including standards for milk, so that dairies that produce milk organically will be able to sell it as organic.

◆ Write to your local dairy companies to find out what their policies and standards are and to express your concerns about the safety of the products you purchase.

CHAPTER 4

MEAT,
POULTRY,
& EGGS

MEAT, POULTRY, & EGGS

Meat makes up a major part of the average American diet—to the tune of some 50 pounds of chicken and 64 pounds of beef for each of us every year. If you're a meat-eater, you should know about some of the problems with the way livestock and poultry are raised and processed—and about how to ensure that your meat and poultry are as safe as possible. For starters, your healthiest choices are to substitute fish, poultry without skin, and lean meat for fatty meats; to trim your meat very carefully; and to eat meat in smaller and fewer portions than is customary in the United States. (See page 204 for some excellent sources of information on vegetarian diets.)

As for eggs, because egg yolks are very high in cholesterol, your consumption of whole eggs should be kept to a minimum, and certainly no more than three per week. When you do eat eggs, be sure to handle and cook them properly to avoid bacterial infection. We'll tell you how. In addition, the Safe Food Choices beginning on page 106 include dozens of tips to take when you choose, handle, and cook meat and poultry to reduce your exposure to potentially harmful bacteria and residues of pesticides and veterinary drugs.

But first: The next time you feel like sinking your teeth into a rare, juicy steak—or the next time you find yourself reaching for a glass of homemade eggnog—consider the following.

FROM FACTORY-FARM TO YOU
PART 1: BUGS

Of the major types of disease-causing bacteria and parasites found in food, almost all have been found in meat or poultry (see "Meet the bugs!" page 94). One out of every 10,000 eggs is likely to be contaminated with salmonella. So if you're like most people, and eat 200 eggs per year, your chances of encountering an egg contaminated with salmonella are high—about one in 50 every year.

Anyone who has ever experienced food poisoning, with its diarrhea and vomiting, knows how debilitating it can be. You've probably had mild bouts of food poisoning without even knowing it. Just a small dose of food-borne bacteria can cause bloating, cramps, nausea, fever, flatulence, constipation, or flu-like symptoms. In more serious cases, bacteria can disrupt intestinal functioning, leading to malnutrition or immune-system problems. And food poisoning can even cause kidney or heart disease, certain kinds of arthritis, or death.[1] In one large outbreak, about 2 percent of the patients developed a chronic reactive arthritis condition within two weeks that was linked to infection with salmonella. Unfortunately, food poisoning in general, and salmonella poisoning in particular, are increasing. And meat, poultry, and eggs are often the culprits.

By all accounts, poultry in the United States is commonly contaminated with salmonella. The USDA says that about a third of raw chickens are contaminated with salmonella, but other experts cite contamination in as many as 50 to 90 percent of chickens leaving some plants.

In 1990, when researchers at the University of Wisconsin screened more than 2,300 laying hens from three flocks, they found only eight birds that were not infected with

Good eggs

Especially if you live in the eastern United States, avoid raw eggs and dishes made with raw eggs, such as homemade eggnog, ice cream, Caesar salad dressing, and mayonnaise. Commercially prepared versions are okay, since they're made with pasteurized eggs. But go easy on them anyway, since they are high in fat and cholesterol.

campylobacter, another bacterium that commonly causes food poisoning.[2]

From 1985 through 1988, state health departments reported 140 outbreaks of *Salmonella enteritidis* affecting nearly 5,000 people, 896 of whom were hospitalized. In almost three-quarters of these outbreaks, Grade A shell eggs were to blame. Things have gotten so bad that *Salmonella enteritidis* infections are now considered an epidemic in New England and the mid-Atlantic states. Even foods containing a single egg contaminated with *Salmonella enteritidis* can cause an outbreak involving severe illness, if that egg is used in a food eaten by a number of people.[3]

You might assume that eggs become contaminated with salmonella through cracks in the shells. They can, but they can also become contaminated directly from the mother hen before the egg shell is formed—which was how eggs implicated in the recent surge of outbreaks were contaminated. So avoid raw eggs—even clean, uncracked Grade A eggs.

The bugs themselves aren't the only cause for concern. If you become infected, your illness will be more difficult to treat if the bacteria happen to be of a strain that is resistant to antibiotics.

FROM FACTORY-FARM TO YOU
PART 2: DRUGS

More than 40 years ago, a scientist at American Cyanamid made a discovery that would help revolutionize meat and poultry production in America: baby chicks given feed that contained traces of the company's new antibiotic drug, chlortetracycline, gained 10 to 20 percent more weight than chicks fed a normal diet. Pigs fed antibiotic-laced feed had even more impressive growth rates.

Antibiotic feed additives first went on sale in the early 1950s. Today, about half of the more than 31 million pounds of antibiotics that are produced annually in the United States is used in animal feed.[4] Antibiotics are routinely fed to about 80 percent of poultry and 75 percent of pigs.[5] In 1985, the National Cattlemen's Association recommended against using antibiotics in cattle feed, but they're probably still being used for some cattle.

Why routine, low doses of antibiotics improve growth rates in livestock is a mystery to scientists. But the drugs do that, and more. By preventing many of the diseases that can result from confining large numbers of animals in production facilities, the routine, low-level use of antibiotics has made factory-type farming possible.[6]

However, the practice may also lead to serious problems for humans. It isn't so much a matter of these antibiotic drug residues ending up in the meat we eat. Instead, the problem is that over time, this daily dosing of livestock with antibiotics creates antibiotic-resistant bacteria, which can spell trouble if they directly infect humans or if this resistance is transferred to other bacteria in the environment or in people. "The problems we're creating with this chronic, low-level antibiotic use are subtle, insidious, and often intractable," says Karim Ahmed, Ph.D., formerly research director with the Natural Resources Defense Council, and currently a private scientific consultant.

Here's why antibiotic resistance is a concern: Only a few effective antibiotics are available for treating some very serious infections. If you happen to get one of those infections, and it is caused by bacteria that are resistant to these antibiotics, the results could be fatal. That's the worst case. A more common scenario might go like this: You eat antibiotic-resistant, disease-causing bacteria in, say, undercooked hamburger, which makes you sick. You then go to the doctor to be treated with an antibiotic, but the antibiotic your doctor first prescribes might not work,

Meet the bugs!
Bacteria

Salmonella. Salmonella causes more than 40,000 reported illnesses a year, but experts believe that the actual number of cases is between 400,000 and 4 million cases annually. And the numbers are growing. Nearly half the reported salmonella infections require hospitalization, and 1 to 2 percent of reported cases result in death. The symptoms of salmonella poisoning range from none to serious illness, such as meningitis. Most often it causes gastroenteritis (inflammation of the stomach or intestines), with symptoms of nausea and diarrhea. Extremely low levels of salmonella, even a single organism, can cause disease. Salmonella infections in AIDS patients are increasing rapidly—salmonellosis is the ninth most common diagnosis in San Francisco AIDS patients.[7]

Campylobacter. Campylobacter is the leading cause of acute gastroenteritis in humans, and raw milk and poultry are the most common causes (which is one reason the FDA has banned the interstate sale of raw milk). Campylobacter has also been found in cake icing, eggs, beef, and even municipal drinking water, usually as a result of fecal contamination. It doesn't take many organisms to cause infection.

E. coli. Escherichia coli, which exists naturally in the human intestinal tract, is the most common cause of diarrhea in infants and travelers. One uncommon strain of E. coli, called 0157:H7, causes two life-threatening conditions: hemorrhagic colitis (marked by severe abdominal cramps followed by bloody diarrhea), and hemolytic uremic syndrome (the leading cause of acute kidney failure in children). Raw and undercooked ground beef and raw milk have been the only foods linked to these illnesses so far, although 0157:H7 E. coli bacteria have also been identified in pork, lamb, and chicken from grocery stores. The bacteria can be controlled by cooking meat thoroughly and avoiding cross-contamination of raw food.

Staphylococcus. Staphylococcus is found in the nose and throat and on the skin of healthy people, as well as on infected cuts and pimples. The bacteria multiply at warm temperatures to produce a toxin that causes illness. Thorough cooking can kill staph, but the toxin is resistant to mild heat, refrigeration, and freezing. You can help control staph by washing your hands and utensils before preparing or serving food, and promptly refrigerating leftovers in shallow, covered containers.

Listeria. Listeria bacteria are common throughout the environment. Most people exposed to listeria experience only mild, flu-like symptoms. But listeria can be deadly to fetuses and newborns, and to people with weakened immune systems. Listeria is estimated to cause at least 1,700 serious infections, and contribute to about 450 deaths and 100 stillbirths each year.[8] It is a tough bug that can grow at refrigeration temperatures and can survive mild heat.

Yersinia. One type of yersinia causes the plague; another type has been linked to food-borne illnesses, the symptoms for which are often mistaken for appendicitis. Like listeria, yersinia can grow at refrigeration temperatures—but unlike listeria, it is not very heat resistant. Yersinia is readily destroyed in milk by normal pasteurization. The yersinia strains that cause illness in people are most frequently found in pork.

Clostridium botulinum. Clostridium botulinum bacteria are present throughout the environment. Botulism is very rare, but the overall fatality rate is high—about 8 percent. Unlike the usual gastrointestinal symptoms of food poisoning, the most common symptoms of botulism are fatigue and blurred vision. Botulism caused by food in damaged cans or by home-canned food is decreasing, but it has been associated with a variety of other foods. Outbreaks have been linked to potato salad, sauteed onions, chopped garlic, raw cabbage, and hazelnut yogurt, among other things. Infant botulism, a very serious disease, can be caused by honey, which often contains botulinum bacteria. Never give honey to an infant under one year old. The honey industry has opposed CSPI's request for labels on honey warning, "Do not feed to infants." (If you can foods at home, see page 190 for how to order information on avoiding botulism.)

Parasites

Trichinella. Cases of trichinosis are declining, and are mostly associated with eating game, such as wild boar or bear, or other non-commercial meats. But still be careful to cook pork thoroughly—to an internal temperature of 160 degrees F—and to be wary of homemade pork sausage.

Toxoplasmosis. Toxoplasmosis is a common parasitic infection in cats. It can be transferred directly to humans through cat feces, or indirectly through improperly cooked meat or poultry. (Animals can get the infection from cats on the farm; at home it can spread from an infected cat to meat.) Infants who acquire the parasite from their mothers before birth can face severe health hazards, such as mental retardation. Toxoplasmosis can be controlled by cooking meat, particularly lamb and pork, thoroughly. Pregnant women should wash their hands after touching cats, and should have someone else change the cat litter box.

and the antibiotic-resistant bacteria are able to multiply to levels that could make you seriously ill. In addition, it takes a smaller dose of antibiotic-resistant bacteria to make you sick if you've recently taken an antibiotic for another infection. That's because the antibiotic may have killed off the normal, sensitive bacteria in your system, leaving the field wide open for the antibiotic-resistant bacteria to multiply to levels that could make you sick.

Because of concerns about antibiotic resistance, several European countries banned the routine use of antibiotics in livestock feed in the 1970s. In the United States, in 1977, the FDA proposed halting the routine use of penicillin and tetracycline in animal feeds. The FDA commissioner at the time called the proposal "the first step toward FDA's ultimate goal of eliminating, to the extent possible, the non-therapeutic use in animals of any drugs needed to treat disease in man." But after intense lobbying by the drug and livestock industries, Congress intervened and told the FDA not to act until more evidence was found about the risk to humans. Since then, between the FDA dragging its feet and Congress asking for more studies, nothing has been done to solve the problem, despite the well-documented dangers:[9]

➤ In 1984 the Centers for Disease Control (CDC) traced an outbreak of antibiotic-resistant salmonella infections in the Midwest—in which one person was killed and 11 others were hospitalized—to hamburger from a herd of cattle that was fed low levels of antibiotics.[10]

➤ When the CDC investigated a 1985 California outbreak of salmonellosis that affected 1,000 people, it tracked an antibiotic-resistant strain of salmonella in 45 of those people to hamburger. The meat came from farms where the cattle had been treated with chloramphenicol, an illegal and dangerous drug. Half the victims in that outbreak were hospitalized, and two died.[11]

➤ Human infections caused by antibiotic-resistant salmonella are increasing. Although this may be in part because of overuse of antibiotics in humans, some scientists believe that the cause is the heavy use of antibiotic drugs on animals.[12] In 1988, the National Academy of Sciences concluded that the magnitude of the antibiotic-resistance problem was uncertain, but it estimated that some 70 human deaths each year might result from the subtherapeutic use of just penicillin and tetracycline in animals.[13]

Antibiotic-resistant bacteria aren't the only problem caused by veterinary drugs. Residues of some drugs used to treat sick animals (including nitrofurazone and other nitrofurans, and sulfamethazine and other sulfa drugs) may slightly increase the risk of cancer or other serious diseases. In the early 1980s, there was widespread illegal use in animals of the drug chloramphenicol. This drug was banned from use in food animals because it has caused aplastic anemia, a fatal disease, when the drug was given to some people. (By the late 1980s, the government said that the use of chloramphenicol in animals had dropped sharply.)[14]

According to USDA tests, veal and pork are much more likely than poultry or beef to contain illegal drug

---

Drugs in your food

Veterinary drugs are used on every type of food-producing animal, from chickens and goats to beef cattle and hogs. In 1985, a congressional subcommittee concluded that "[FDA] officials believe that as many as 90 percent or more of the 20,000 to 30,000 new animal drugs estimated to be on the market have not been approved by FDA as safe and effective and, therefore, are being marketed in violation of the...Food, Drug, and Cosmetic Act. It is estimated that as many as 4,000 of these new animal drugs may have 'potentially significant adverse effects on animals or humans.'"[15]

residues. In pork, the most common problem reported is illegal levels of sulfamethazine. And veal has the highest overall rate of illegal drug residues: in 1989 almost 3 percent of veal carcasses tested were found to contain illegal levels of antibiotics and sulfa drugs.

The Animal Health Institute (AHI), an industry trade association, says that in 1989 alone, farmers spent over $2.5 billion on pharmaceuticals, feed additives, and other veterinary drugs. AHI estimates that these animal drugs reduce the cost of meat, poultry, dairy products, and eggs by about 9 percent. But the question is: Is it worth the risks to our health?

The good news about drugs in animals is that the misuse of growth hormones in cattle appears to be under control. Hormones, which are implanted in cattle's ears to keep them out of edible cuts of meat, have been used for years to produce leaner, cheaper beef. In Europe, growth hormones in livestock were banned in 1988, after reports from Italy linking hormone misuse with cases of premature sexual development. (There were similar reports in Puerto Rico in 1985.) In the United States, most of the hormones remain legal, and two out of every three cattle are implanted with them, according to the National Cattlemen's Association. Even European scientists agree that there is no evidence that the hormones are unsafe as long as they are used properly.

In 1979, the FDA banned the most controversial growth hormone, DES, from use in cattle after researchers linked a rare vaginal cancer to the daughters of women who had taken large doses of DES during pregnancy to prevent miscarriage. Although illegal use of DES in livestock continued into the early 1980s, violations have since dropped off. But in 1986, some cattle feedlots were at it again. The USDA caught them implanting pellets of the hormones zeranol and estradiol in the brisket and other edible portions of cattle. But such widespread problems haven't been found since then.

The USDA hasn't played a very admirable role in the whole hormone controversy, however. It was furious when Europe cut off imports of most American beef. Incredibly enough, the USDA at first sought to stop Texas from marketing hormone-free meat, but the agency ultimately relented.

Today the hormones-in-meat controversy has been overshadowed by the BGH/BST-in-milk controversy (see page 83). Meanwhile, biotechnologists have begun producing another hormone that may hit the headlines soon. This hormone is porcine somatotropin, or PST, a growth hormone that helps produce lower-fat pork. That's a terrific nutritional advantage, but whether PST is ultimately approved and used on farms will depend on its safety to both humans and hogs. Stay tuned.

FROM FACTORY-FARM TO YOU
PART 3: PESTICIDES AND CONTAMINANTS

Accidents will happen. They happen in our homes, they happened in Chernobyl and Bhopal, and they happen on farms. In several incidents, in fact, the accidental (and occasionally deliberate) misuse of chemicals or pesticides has led to massive contamination of farm animals and food supplies:

➤ In 1973, farmers in Michigan were sold bags of what they thought was a livestock feed supplement. The bags turned out to contain chemical fire-retardants called PBBs (polybrominated biphenyls), which are possible human carcinogens. The mix-up happened at the feed-mixing plant. The result was widespread contamination of meat and dairy products. The food reached consumers before the problem was discovered, and high levels of PBBs, along with evidence of immune-system abnormalities, were later found in the blood and tissues of many dairy farmers and local residents.[16]

➤ In 1988, residues of chlordane—a carcinogenic pesticide banned in food—were found in several flocks of broiler chickens in Maryland. The contamination was traced to a farm where chlordane had been illegally applied to the inside of a grain-storage bin containing 4,500 bushels of feed corn. Fortunately, the problem was discovered before the chickens reached the market.[17]

➤ In 1989, one of the nation's largest poultry producers had to destroy 400,000 chickens because they were contaminated with the cancer-causing pesticide heptachlor. Although heptachlor was banned for use in food crops in 1978, the EPA continues to allow existing supplies to be used to treat grain seeds. In this incident, sorghum seeds were treated with heptachlor, and then sold illegally as feed grain. It wasn't the federal government that discovered the problem, but the Campbell Soup Company, which had bought 200 pounds of meat for test runs of a new product, and discovered the contamination in routine pesticide testing.[18]

When we think of pesticide residues in food, we usually think of fruits and vegetables. Since produce is monitored by the FDA, and meat by the USDA, it's difficult to directly compare contamination levels in these different foods. But a 1988 Canadian study indicates that meat may be more contaminated than we would think. When researchers there looked at organochlorine contaminants (which include PCBs, lindane, and various chlorobenzenes), they found the highest contamination in the "meat and eggs" category.[19] Organochlorine contaminants accumulate in fat.

FROM FACTORY-FARM TO YOU
PART 4: REGULATION AND INSPECTION

How well do government programs work to ensure meat safety? Reports by the U.S. Congress,[20] the General Accounting Office,[21] the Office of Technology Assessment,[22] the USDA Inspector General,[23] and the National Academy of Sciences[24] are not very reassuring:

➤ The USDA's Food Safety and Inspection Service (FSIS) routinely uses tests designed to detect only 40 (18 percent) of the 227 pesticide ingredients it considers to be of potential concern. The FSIS has identified 10 pesticides that are "highly ranked" (according to their toxicity and levels of human exposure) that it would like to monitor routinely in meat but doesn't. What's more, even when it does find contamination, the FSIS does not stop contaminated food from reaching the market.

➤ Allowable levels of pesticides and animal drugs are not necessarily "safe" levels. The USDA Inspector General found that the FSIS had no support for 4 of the 12 "action levels" used to regulate pesticide residues found in red meat and poultry—and that, as a result, "FSIS had no assurance that these pesticides were being monitored at levels necessary to protect the public health."

➤ Various agricultural by-products (such as citrus pulp and almond hulls) that may contain pesticide residues are fed to animals. But the EPA has not set maximum legal limits for such residues in by-products used for animal feed.

➤ In 1985, the Committee on Government Operations of the U.S. House of Representatives found that the FDA's "extra-label-use" policy (which allows the use of veterinary drugs for unapproved purposes) violates federal law and makes illegal drug residues in food more likely to go undetected by the USDA's routine monitoring program. In addition, the FDA hasn't been able to control

Food irradiation

For decades, some food experts have urged the use of radiation to kill germs and insects, including treating poultry to kill salmonella. Advocates of this technology claim that it could lead to cheaper and safer food, less hunger, and reduced use of dangerous pesticides.

Food irradiation has been approved in the United States for use on various foods, including flour, spices, fruit and vegetables, and poultry. But you probably won't find any irradiated food in your supermarket—except perhaps some irradiated spices. The reason: consumers and food producers don't want it. In fact, General Foods, PepsiCo, Perdue Chicken, and other processors have all pledged not to sell irradiated foods, and a few states have passed temporary bans on the sale of irradiated foods.

Several decades of research on irradiation and irradiated foods have produced dozens of studies, but they haven't proved conclusively that irradiated food is safe—or unsafe. Irradiation does not cause food to be radioactive. But irradiation forms new chemical compounds in food called "unique radiolytic products." The FDA maintains that many of these chemicals are identical or similar to chemicals formed during other forms of cooking. To test them properly, each one of these substances would need to be identified and fed in large quantities to laboratory animals to determine if it caused mutations, cancer, liver damage, or other problems. But such tests would be so costly that they will never be conducted, and so scientists may never be able to prove to the most severe critics that irradiation is absolutely safe.

The most serious problems surrounding irradiation may have more to do with occupational and environmental risks than with food safety. Irradiation requires more transport of radioactive materials on busy roadways, puts more workers at risk of exposure to low-level radiation, and adds to the hazardous-waste disposal problem.

In the case of poultry, irradiation would be a band-aid solution to a serious problem. Better, more fundamental ways exist to control bacteria—including improved production, slaughtering, and processing methods, and better government inspection. In other cases, alternative methods are often cheaper and easier.

What you can do as a citizen

◆ Make your feelings about irradiation known to grocers and manufacturers.

◆ Insist on clear labeling. Currently, foods that are irradiated must be labeled with a "radura" symbol (resembling a flower—see below) and the words "treated with irradiation." The FDA should also require that irradiated ingredients in processed foods be so labeled in the ingredients list, and restaurants should disclose their use of irradiated foods.

◆ Call on Congress to ask the National Academy of Sciences to review the basis on which the safety of irradiation has been judged.

◆ Demand that the government regularly inspect food irradiation facilities, and develop methods for determining if and how heavily food has been irradiated.

the illegal sales of veterinary drugs. And even for approved veterinary drugs, human food-safety data is inadequate for the majority of drugs in use.

➤ The FSIS has no on-farm inspection authority. Most illegal contamination comes from misuse of pesticides and veterinary drugs on the farm, but the USDA's inspection authority is limited to the slaughterhouse.

The processing methods used to turn animals into the food you buy at the store are unsanitary and can lead to the spread of bacterial infection. For instance, chickens are "defeathered" by a machine that holds and plucks the chickens while pressing bacteria-laden feces out of the freshly killed birds. This ends up soiling the "rubber fingers" that pluck the feathers. As they work, these "fingers" then beat the feces into the chickens' skin, especially into the empty follicles that held the feathers. After the birds are defeathered and eviscerated, they are plunged into a bath of icy water, which can also spread bacteria from one bird to another.

Rodney Leonard, a former USDA official who now is executive director of the Community Nutrition Institute, recommends that USDA require chicken slaughter plants to remove the chickens' skins, "the most likely source of food poisoning from poultry."

Meat and poultry inspection in general is seriously inadequate. By law, federal inspectors at meat and poultry processing plants have to visually inspect every carcass. But depending on the speed of processing lines—chickens can whiz by inspectors at the rate of 90 per minute—inspectors have only about two seconds or less to examine each bird.

What's more, visual inspection can't even detect most bacterial infections or chemical contamination. In 1987, the National Academy of Sciences concluded that "current poultry inspection procedures, which emphasize bird-by-bird visual and manual examination, cannot detect the most important types of microbial or chemical contamination and therefore cannot provide effective protection for public health."[25]

Inspection of cattle is not much better. And the USDA has proposed a "streamlined inspection system" (SIS) for inspecting cattle that threatens to undermine meat safety even more. The SIS program is already being tested at five meat-packing plants (the USDA has to notify Congress if it plans to expand the program). Under SIS, many of the inspection procedures formerly followed by federal inspectors are done by plant workers instead. Federal inspectors have just 12 seconds to examine each cattle carcass. And they aren't permitted to look at internal organs, even though that is the only way to detect and diagnose many diseases.

What's more, inspectors have no authority to control problems such as fecal contamination, which is the primary cause of food poisoning. As one inspector said, "To put it simply, under SIS we have lost faith in the USDA seal of approval. In good conscience, we no longer can say that we know USDA-approved beef is wholesome." As another inspector put it, "We wouldn't want our friends and families to eat some of the stuff that routinely gets by now."

The USDA is currently attempting to develop a new system, called Hazard Analysis and Critical Control Point (HACCP) for inspecting meat and poultry. There are several problems with the new system. One is that the USDA has rejected making microbiological standards for raw poultry and meat part of the system. Therefore, it is unlikely to be very effective in reducing food poisoning. Further, the new system will rely primarily on plant employees to prevent and report unsanitary conditions. Unlike federal inspectors, these plant employees are not covered by so-called "whistle-blower" protection and can be fired if they report violations of health standards.

SAFE FOOD CHOICES

AT THE MARKET

◆ Shop for meat, poultry, and eggs last, and refrigerate them as soon as possible, but at least within two hours. If you live in a warm climate, and it will take you longer than one hour from the store to your refrigerator, bring an ice chest along and pack these items in it for the trip home.

◆ Buy eggs only if they have been refrigerated in the store. (Keeping raw eggs at room temperature allows salmonella to grow to high concentrations.) Choose grade AA or A eggs, which are required to have clean, uncracked shells. It's a good idea to open the carton and inspect eggs in the store to avoid buying eggs with any cracks—even small cracks.

◆ Choose the safest and leanest cuts of meat. To reduce fat in your diet, choose chicken without the skin over red meat, or choose the leanest meats, such as round steak, sirloin, and pork tenderloin, trimmed meticulously. ("Lean" and "extra lean" ground beef are not really lean.) Eat only small amounts, if any, of kidney, liver, and other organ meats, because of their high cholesterol content and because many veterinary drugs concentrate in these organs.

◆ Look for meat and poultry raised without antibiotics or other feed additives. These products are available in many stores, from small specialty food shops to some major supermarket chains. Look for "raising claim" labels that explicitly state that the meat is raised without antibiotic or other feed additives—USDA policy allows meat and poultry to be labeled "natural" even if they contain drug and pesticide residues. The catch: antibiotic-free meats are usually more expensive than other meat and poultry.

◆ Buy packaged meats only if the packaging has no tears or punctures. Also, buy only products that were properly stored in refrigeration, and never buy anything for which the sell-by or use-by date has expired.

◆ To avoid spreading any salmonella or other bacteria that may be in meat, keep packages of raw meat and poultry separate from other foods—especially foods that you'll be eating without further cooking. Place raw meat or poultry in your shopping cart in a way that will keep meat fluids from dripping on other foods, and make sure that meat and poultry are bagged separately from other food on the way home.

◆ If you order meat and poultry by mail, it must arrive at your door as cold as if it were refrigerated. When you order by mail, ask whether a cooling source will be included in the package. If it is not cold when it arrives, call the mail-order company to arrange for a refund or a replacement that will arrive cold.

IN YOUR KITCHEN

Safe storage

◆ Refrigerate or freeze raw meat and poultry, and refrigerate eggs immediately when you get home. Refrigeration and even freezing won't kill harmful bacteria, but they can keep them from multiplying. In your refrigerator, store raw meat and poultry on a plate or in a container (even if they are packaged) to keep them from dripping on other food or on refrigerator shelves. Since repeated handling can introduce bacteria, don't

Angeled eggs

In eggs, it's the yolk that has the high cholesterol content—the egg white contains no cholesterol. (Salmonella is found in both the white and the yolk, but it grows more quickly in the yolk.) In recipes that call for more than one egg, use one whole egg, and substitute just the egg whites for the other eggs.

And try this recipe for "angeled" eggs: boil eggs for at least seven minutes; peel and slice in half lengthwise; discard the yolk; and fill the cavity with a mixture of drained, rinsed, water-packed tuna, finely chopped onion, and a bit of nonfat yogurt or "light" or fat-free mayonnaise.

The big thaw

With turkey, as with other poultry and meat, thawing on your countertop isn't a good idea, since that creates perfect conditions for bacteria to flourish. (While the center of the turkey is still frozen, the outer part reaches room temperature, allowing bacteria to multiply.) Here's how the USDA recommends thawing a turkey safely:

◆ **In the refrigerator.** Allow the following thawing times: one to two days for an 8- to 12-pound turkey; two to three days for a 12- to 16-pound turkey; three to four days for a 16- to 20-pound turkey; four to five days for a 20- to 24-pound turkey.

◆ **In cold water.** First, check the wrapping to make sure there are no tears. (If the original wrapping is torn, put the turkey in another plastic bag and close it securely.) Place the turkey in its unopened bag in the sink or a large container, and cover it with cold water. Change the water frequently—at least every 30 minutes. For an 8- to 12-pound turkey, allow 4 to 6 hours for thawing; for a 12- to 16-pound turkey, allow 6 to 9 hours; for a 16- to 20-pound turkey, allow 9 to 11 hours; for a 20- to 24-pound turkey, allow 11 to 12 hours.

Once the turkey is thawed, remove the neck and giblets from the neck and body cavities; wash the giblets and the inside and outside of the turkey in cold water, and drain well.

If you're buying fresh, unfrozen turkey, choose one that has been properly refrigerated at the store—avoid any turkeys that are stacked above the top of the store's refrigerator case. At home, either freeze it or refrigerate it and use it within one or two days.

remove the store wrapping unless it's torn. Unless you freeze it, the USDA recommends that you use fresh meat within three to five days, fresh poultry within one to two days, and ground beef and stew meats within one to two days. Make sure your refrigerator temperature is 40 degrees F or colder, and your freezer 0 degrees or below.

◆ Store eggs in your refrigerator in their original cartons, not in egg trays on the refrigerator door, where they'll be jostled and can develop microscopic cracks. Don't wash eggs before storing them. Most eggs sold commercially have been washed and sanitized. This washing removes the protective oil that is found naturally on eggs, so processors often replace it with a thin coating of edible mineral oil. Washing eggs at home will remove this protective coating, and bacteria present on the shells can invade the egg through the pores.

◆ Use raw eggs within three weeks and hard-cooked eggs within a week. Since cooking destroys the protective cuticle of the eggshell, a hard-cooked egg is more vulnerable to contamination than a raw egg and can't be safely

---

Well done, eggs!

Always cook eggs and egg-rich foods until the yolk is set, not runny, and the white is firm. Cook scrambled eggs until firm. If your stove has a temperature control, pre-heat it to 250 degrees F and observe these cooking times:

◆ Scrambled: 1 minute

◆ Sunny-side up: 7 minutes, or covered for 4 minutes

◆ Fried or over easy: 3 minutes on one side, 2 on the other

Cook boiled eggs in boiling water as follows:

◆ Poached: 5 minutes

◆ Hard-boiled: 7 to 10 minutes

stored as long. Leftover whites and yolks should be used within two to four days. You can safely eat hard-cooked eggs that you have used in an Easter egg hunt, as long as they haven't been out of the refrigerator for more than two hours.

◆ Refrigerate or freeze all cooked leftovers in small, covered, shallow containers (to allow them to cool quickly). Refrigerate food within two hours after cooking if the room temperature is 90 degrees F or cooler, within one hour if it is warmer. Throw out perishable food that's been at room temperature for more than two hours.

Safe handling and preparation

◆ As a general rule, treat raw meat, poultry, and eggs as if they were contaminated. Chances are good that they are. Keep raw meat and poultry, and their juices, out of contact with other food, raw or cooked. And any time you handle raw meat, poultry, or eggs, wash your hands, utensils, and surfaces thoroughly with hot, soapy water. Wear rubber gloves if you have any kind of cut or infection on your hands (and wash the gloves as thoroughly as you would your bare hands). Use a dish cloth to clean kitchen surfaces (not a sponge, which can harbor bacteria), and switch to a clean one after working with raw meat, poultry, or eggs. Cut raw meat and poultry on a plastic or other nonporous cutting board that can be cleaned thoroughly after each use; a wooden cutting board may be too porous to clean well. While you're cooking, don't taste any raw or undercooked meat, poultry, or eggs.

◆ Thaw frozen meat and poultry only in the refrigerator, in cold water changed at least every 30 minutes, or in a microwave oven. Cook foods thawed in a microwave immediately after thawing. Food that has been thawed in the refrigerator can be safely refrozen.

Now you're cookin'

The trick to cooking meat safely is to cook it thoroughly, in order to kill bacteria or parasites—but to avoid overcooking, which can cause the formation of suspected cancer-causing chemicals called HAs (heterocyclic amines). Based on preliminary assessments, the National Cancer Institute estimates that HAs may increase the number of human cancers in the United States by about 2,000 cases per year. HAs form most readily when meat, poultry, or fish are cooked at high temperatures for a long time. To reduce your exposure to HAs:

◆ Precook meat, poultry, and fish in a microwave on "High" for 30 to 90 seconds, and discard the juice that collects. That removes some of the "starting materials" necessary for HAs to form. Then immediately cook it in the conventional oven, on the grill, or as you normally would.

◆ Don't make gravy from meat drippings.

◆ Keep a few inches between the heat and the meat when broiling. And use as low a temperature and as little oil as possible when pan frying. Frying and broiling produce the greatest amounts of HAs; oven roasting, baking, and stewing produce fewer. This is because of the higher temperatures required for frying and broiling.

◆ Buy a meat thermometer, and use it correctly. Put it into the thickest part of the meat, but not so that it touches any bone, fat, or gristle. You can insert the thermometer either before you cook the meat, or at the end of cooking—just be sure to wait until the mercury stops moving. (If you're using a microwave oven, use the thermometer after cooking, and test several spots, since microwaves can cook food unevenly.) The USDA recommends cooking meat to the following internal temperatures:

beef—160° F   **veal**—170° F
lamb—170° F   **pork**—170° F
poultry—180 to 185° F   **stuffing**—165° F
boneless turkey roast—170 to 175° F

Grilling safely to avoid natural carcinogens

Barbecuing may be one of those great American pastimes, but it is not entirely safe. Whenever fat drips onto a flame, heating element, or hot coals during grilling, suspected cancer-causing chemicals called PAHs (polycyclic aromatic hydrocarbons) form. They rise with the smoke and are deposited on the food's surface. They can also form directly on the food when it's charred. Back in the 1700s, PAH-containing soot was linked to cancer in chimney sweeps—today, grilled meat is the major source of PAHs in food.

If you eat grilled meats only once in a blue moon, your risk is minimal. But if you enjoy grilled foods regularly, you can do several things to make your grilling safer:

◆ **Keep fat from dripping onto the heat source and producing smoke.** Use a drip pan, wrap meats in foil, or grill the meats to one side of (not directly over) the coals. Increase the distance between the heat source and meat. If the results don't produce enough of that "charcoal-broiled" taste, try a little liquid smoke. You'll get fewer PAHs that way.

◆ **Grill vegetables instead of meat.**

◆ **Cut the fat.** Select the least fatty cuts of meat, or choose fish or poultry instead of beef or pork. Remove skin and trim off fat before cooking.

◆ **Keep oil in marinades to a minimum.** You can use barbecue sauce or low-fat salad dressing for basting instead.

◆ **Discard the drippings** formed during grilling.

◆ **Avoid charring meats.** Grill only properly thawed meat; otherwise the outside may char while the inside remains frozen. Cut away any charred parts before eating.

◆ **Use regular charcoal.** Mesquite or other soft woods burn at a higher temperature and form more PAHs than regular charcoal, which is made from hardwood. (Using a gas grill doesn't prevent PAHs from forming— follow the above steps.)

Keep the environment in mind when you grill, too. Charcoal-lighter fluid creates smog-forming emissions— so many that Los Angeles is considering banning It unless manufacturers of lighter fluid and self-starting briquets can develop products that meet strict new air-quality standards. Try one of the charcoal-starter products that doesn't require lighter fluid. You place the charcoal in a narrow upright cylinder, and light the charcoal with a match. The cylinder controls the air flow, and in about 15 minutes you've got blazing hot coals ready to dump into your grill. Or switch to a gas grill.

◆ Residues of some pesticides concentrate in animal fat, so trim fat from meat and poultry, and the skin (which contains most of the fat) from poultry. Discard fats and oil in broths and pan drippings.

◆ Marinate raw products in the refrigerator, not on the counter—and serve the marinade only if you cook it thoroughly to destroy any bacteria that may have accumulated there from the raw meat.

◆ Stuff raw poultry just before cooking it—never the night before. Keep frozen prestuffed poultry frozen until cooking it, and carefully follow the package instructions for storing and cooking. Use a conventional oven for cooking stuffed poultry; a microwave oven may not cook it thoroughly. Consider cooking poultry and stuffing separately; it takes less time, and you have better control over the cooking. If you do stuff poultry, remove all of the stuffing immediately after cooking and put it in a bowl for serving. Never store leftover poultry with the stuffing inside. (It will take so long to cool that bacteria will have time to multiply.)

Safe cooking

◆ Avoid any recipes that call for cooking without a heat source (such as boiling water, then putting in poultry and turning the burner off, or preheating your oven to 500 degrees, inserting a roast, and then turning off the oven). Cook food without interruption, since interrupting cooking can allow bacteria to multiply in warm food.

◆ Proper cooking kills harmful bacteria in meat and poultry. Use a meat thermometer for meat and poultry more than two inches thick (see "Now you're cookin'" on page 111 for temperatures). For meat and poultry less than two inches thick, look for clear juices and lack of pink in the center as signs of doneness.

◆ Don't put cooked meat or poultry back on a plate containing raw juices.

◆ Always cook hot dogs thoroughly—uncooked hot dogs have been implicated in listeria infections.

◆ Use special care when microwaving meat and poultry; see page 187. In conventional ovens, use a temperature of at least 325 degrees F. And if you use a slow cooker such as a "crock pot," start with fresh rather than frozen meat or poultry, and smaller chunks rather than roasts or large cuts. Check the internal temperature of meat in several spots to be sure it is thoroughly cooked to 160 degrees or higher.

◆ Cook eggs thoroughly to kill salmonella bacteria. Eggs are safe when cooked until the white is completely firm, and the yolk is beginning to thicken (no longer runny). (For cooking times for eggs, see "Well done, egg!" page 109.) Realize that there may be some risk in eating lightly cooked eggs such as soft-boiled, soft-scrambled, or sunny-side up, or foods such as lightly cooked French toast, mousse, and meringue. People with weakened immune systems should never eat raw eggs or dishes with lightly cooked eggs.

WHAT YOU CAN DO AS A CITIZEN

◆ Ask your grocery store to stock meat, poultry, and eggs raised without pesticides and antibiotics.

◆ Write to your representatives in Congress and urge them to step up meat and poultry inspections to protect the public from bacterial contamination and drug residues. Ask them to require the USDA to add this notice to meat and poultry labels: "Notice: Cook thoroughly to destroy any harmful bacteria that may be present. Wash hands, dishes, and implements with soap and water immediately after contact with raw product." Insist that any new inspection system be rejected unless it includes bacterial standards and "whistle-blower protection" for plant employees who report problems.

◆ Write to the USDA, and ask it to promptly implement new standards for producing meat and poultry
organically.

◆ Write to the FDA and demand that it ban the use
of any cancer-causing veterinary drugs, as well as the routine feeding of antibiotics.

CHAPTER 5
FISH & SHELLFISH

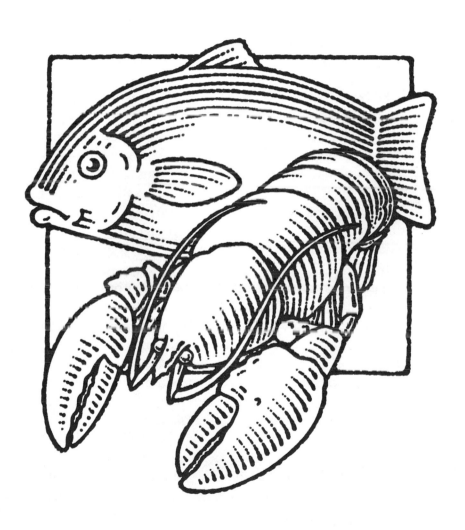

FISH & SHELLFISH

Maybe there's some truth to the signs that you sometimes see in fish markets: "Eat fish, live longer." Fish certainly has a lot to offer: low-fat protein, B vitamins, trace elements, and heart-protecting omega-3 fatty acids—all with very little saturated fat. In fact, people who eat fish one or more times a week have reduced risks of coronary heart disease.

Can anything this good for you ever be bad for you? Yes, unfortunately—if your fish also comes with a hefty dose of natural or unnatural contaminants. But fortunately, you can do several things to minimize your risks. Most fish consumed by Americans, for instance, is deep-sea marine fish, which poses less cancer risk from chemical contamination than freshwater fish.[1] So you're already doing a lot to minimize long-term risks if you eat fish from the deep blue sea instead of freshwater or near-shore fish—especially if you avoid the fattiest fish.

And, if you exercise care in buying, handling, and preparing fish, you can go a long way toward minimizing the risks of microbial contamination, too. Start by avoiding raw shellfish—*no other commercially available food poses a greater health risk*. Never eat raw shellfish if you have AIDS, cancer, diabetes, or liver disease, or if you are a heavy drinker of alcohol. The Safe Food Choices beginning on page 126 spell out in detail the various steps you can take to be sure that the fish you eat is a health boon, not a health risk. But first, a look at some of the problems:

SOMETHING'S FISHY
PART 1: MICROBES AND NATURAL TOXINS

Fish spend their lives in water—and if there's something wrong with the water, chances are something will be wrong with the fish. Whether the problems are caused by human pollution or by natural microbes or toxins, the possibilities for seafood contamination are not pleasant.

From 1983 through 1987, 56 percent of the food-poisoning outbreaks linked to "meat" (including meat, poultry, fish, and shellfish) were due to seafood, even though seafood comprised just 8 percent of the "meat" consumed during that time.[2] Microbes and toxins in shellfish—including oysters, mussels, and clams—cause some 31 percent of the seafood-related outbreaks, and 66 percent of the cases, of food poisoning in the United States.[3] (In measuring occurrences of food poisoning, "cases" refers to the number of individuals affected; "outbreaks" refers to incidences in which there were multiple victims.)

Bacteria and viruses. The greatest number of seafood-related illnesses come from raw molluscan shellfish (oysters, clams, and mussels) harvested in waters contaminated with human sewage. Most of these illnesses are mild cases of stomachache and diarrhea, probably caused

---

Raw-bar conversation stoppers

Molluscan shellfish—oysters, clams, and mussels—obtain food and oxygen from their surroundings by pumping large quantities of water across their gill systems. Oysters can process about 4 quarts an hour, and clams about 3 quarts. Along with the water go whatever bacteria, viruses, natural toxins, and chemical contaminants happen to be in it.

What's more, mollusks have an efficient method of filtration and concentrate microorganisms and metals in their intestines at much higher levels than are found in the water itself. The level of harmful bacteria in a mollusk can be from 3 to 20 times that found in the surrounding water. Federal authorities estimate that one out of every 250 servings of raw or partially cooked shellfish will result in illness.

Your safest bet: don't eat shellfish raw!

---

by viruses such as the Norwalk virus.[4] Seafood can also become contaminated with salmonella or campylobacter bacteria, either from fecal pollution of water or from improper processing or preparation. Vibrio bacteria, which occur naturally in water, are responsible for fewer reported cases of infection from raw shellfish, but vibrio

---

Avoiding natural toxins in seafood

Although cooking won't destroy natural toxins in fish, you can still avoid the risks:

► **Ciguatera,** the most common type of finfish (as opposed to shellfish) poisoning reported in the United States, occurs mainly in Hawaii, Puerto Rico, the Virgin Islands, Guam, and Florida. To play it safe within those areas, avoid certain reef fish, including amber-jack, some snapper species, grouper, goatfish, and barracuda—unless you have reliable information that they were caught from waters unaffected by ciguatoxin. Ciguatoxin is thought to be pro-duced by tiny organisms called dinoflagellates (similar to those that cause "red tide") that fish ingest when they feed on algae.

► **Scombroid (or histamine) fish poisoning** is caused in the United States mainly by mahi-mahi, tuna, and bluefish that haven't been refrigerated properly. Although you can't necessarily smell anything "fishy," the toxin is produced as the fish spoils. It may be more common than ciguatera and simply reported less often since its symptoms are milder. Always purchase fish from a reputable dealer or establishment.

► **Paralytic shellfish poisoning** is less common but more dangerous than either ciguatera or scombroid fish poisoning. It's a problem primarily in the New England coastal states and in Alaska, California, and Washington, and is produced by toxic dinoflagellates. Most paralytic shellfish poisoning incidents involve mussels, clams, and scallops harvested from closed areas. Don't harvest shellfish from closed areas. Do buy shellfish from a rep-utable dealer, not a truck by the side of the road.

vulnificus is particularly deadly for people with liver disease or lowered immunity.

Natural toxins. Fish contaminated with natural toxins from microorganisms that the fish eat or from spoilage can lead to diseases such as ciguatera, scombroid fish poisoning, paralytic shellfish poisoning, and other illnesses caused by shellfish toxins. The symptoms of these diseases range from mild diarrhea, vomiting, and nausea to neurological symptoms such as tingling and numbness, rashes, and respiratory paralysis. A person cannot detect these toxins by smell or by taste, and none of them can be destroyed by normal cooking. Fortunately, the risks of eating contaminated fish are principally limited to certain regions of the country and certain fish species, so they're relatively easy to avoid.

Parasites. As raw-fish dishes such as sushi and sashimi have become more popular, infections from parasitic worms in fish have increased. For instance, anisakiasis is caused by anisakid worms, which can penetrate the lining of the stomach and intestine, causing fever, nausea, and abdominal pain. Although anisakiasis is still uncommon, more than 70 percent of all reported cases in the United States occurred after 1980. Raw Pacific salmon and Pacific rockfish (red snapper) are most frequently linked to the disease.[5]

SOMETHING'S FISHY
PART 2: CHEMICAL CONTAMINATION

Although the monitoring of waters and fish is spotty, evidence indicates that chemical contamination of fish is a serious problem as well. Those who are most at risk from chemical contaminants in fish are people who eat fish they catch themselves, pregnant women, and children.

Pesticides. According to the FDA, fish and seafood products contain pesticide residues more frequently than fruits, vegetables, grains, and dairy products do.[6] Fish accumulate more fat-soluble pesticides (and certain other chemicals) because they're near the top of a long food chain, at each level of which the contaminants become more and more concentrated. The pesticide found most often in fish is DDT, which was banned in 1972. In 1983, the FDA found DDT (a probable human carcinogen) in 334 of the 386 samples of domestic fish it tested.[7] High levels of DDT are still being found in some fish caught in waters off Los Angeles County where DDT used to be manufactured. In a 1989 study, heavy fish eaters who ate locally caught sportfish at least three times a week for three years had DDT levels in their blood five times higher, on average, than people who consumed little or no locally caught fish.[8]

Toxic metals. Lead, cadmium, chromium, and arsenic frequently turn up in shellfish. Excessive exposure to toxic metals can cause health problems ranging from kidney damage and impaired mental development to cancer. High levels of another toxic metal, methyl mercury, have been found in large predatory fish, including swordfish, large tuna, shark, halibut, and marlin. Pregnant women should avoid these and some other types of fish, since fetuses are particularly vulnerable to mercury. (See "Defensive eating," page 12.) Methyl mercury attacks human nerve cells, and can cause numbness and loss of coordination as well as hearing and visual problems.

Clean fish

Cod, haddock, and pollock are safe fish choices. Small tuna is OK, too, but large tuna may have high levels of mercury. Most major commercial brands of canned tuna are monitored to ensure that mercury is below the allowable levels set by the FDA. Even so, if you're pregnant, to play it safe don't eat much tuna.

Farm-raised fish raise new questions

Approximately 12 percent of the fish eaten by Americans today are raised by aquaculture[9]—the breeding, rearing, and harvesting of fish in environmentally-controlled conditions. "Fish farming" is a fast-growing industry, as pollution, over-fishing, and other problems are depleting supplies of fish in the wild. In 1987, about 750 million pounds of fish and shellfish were produced in the United States using aquaculture—up from 203 million pounds in 1980.[10] The types of seafood being produced by aquaculture include catfish, salmon, trout, redfish, sturgeon, hybrid striped bass, carp, tilapia, oysters, and crawfish. Although fish farming conceivably could help avoid chemical contaminants, it can cause problems of its own:

➤ In fish farms, it isn't unusual for a large number of fish to be reared in a small, confined space, which may result in stress-related disease—and the use of drugs to control it. According to the FDA, little is known about the resulting drug residues in fish. The FDA says that while many of the drugs used in fish farming have been in use for years and may be legal for use in other animal species, most haven't been approved for use in aquaculture and don't have established "withdrawal" times to allow the drugs to pass out of the fish before they are sold.[11] In 1988, Argent Chemical Laboratories was found guilty of illegally distributing drugs and pesticides for use by fish farms and fined $70,000.

➤ Of particular concern is the development of antibiotic-resistant strains of bacteria, and the potential transfer of antibiotic-resistant bacteria in seafood to humans. Scientists have already found tetracycline-resistant strains of bacteria in farmed catfish and their environment.[12]

➤ The FDA has expressed concern about the illegal use of color additives in feed to color fish flesh.[13]

➤ Farm-raised fish may have lower levels of the heart-protecting omega-3 fatty acids than are found in wild fish, because of the type of feed used in aquaculture.[14]

Industrial chemicals. The single biggest chemical risk in seafood comes from PCBs, which are carcinogenic and can impair the healthy development of fetuses. In 1984, researchers at Wayne State University and other universities examined infants of women who reported regularly eating an average of two or three meals per week of PCB-contaminated fish from Lake Michigan. At birth, the babies showed weak reflexes and sluggish movements, and other signs of "worrisome" behavior development.[15] The commercially caught fish that contribute the most PCBs to our diets are freshwater fish, sea herring, bluefish, mackerel, sea trout, mullet, porgy, and scup.[16]

Dioxins, which are extremely potent animal carcinogens, pose another problem. Even though some studies suggest that human beings may be less sensitive to dioxins than laboratory animals, levels of just 1 part per trillion (ppt) may slightly increase a person's risk of cancer. Although concern over dioxins in milk has received much more publicity, the levels of dioxins in fish are far higher. The EPA has found dioxin contamination in fish at about 85 sites throughout the United States, in levels up to 41 ppt for fillets and 85 ppt for whole fish. Dioxins were found in fish from the Great Lakes, major river systems such as the Ohio and Mississippi Rivers, and other waterways with significant industrial activity.[17]

The risk from dioxin contamination may be especially high for people eating fish caught downstream from paper mills that use chlorine bleach. The EPA estimated that for one-tenth to one-quarter of these mills, eating just one 4-ounce serving of fish caught downstream could cause liver damage. Eating two servings per month would cause an extremely high increase in a person's lifetime cancer risk.[18]

REGULATION: GONE FISHIN'

What is the federal government doing about all this? Not enough. The FDA and EPA are supposed to establish and enforce maximum allowable levels of toxic substances in fish. But their regulation of contaminants is riddled with problems:

➤ Federal action levels and tolerances are designed to protect "average" consumers, not seafood lovers. The FDA's definition of "average" is pretty stingy, though. For example, the tolerance for PCBs in fish is 2 parts per million. But if, once every 40 days, you ate more than 4 ounces of catfish, carp, buffalo fish, freshwater or sea trout, bass, chubs, bluefish, porgy, drum, or mackerel, you'd be above average.[19]

➤ Many of the FDA limits on contamination in fish are inconsistent with today's scientific standards and should be tightened. A recent study by a National Wildlife Federation scientist concluded that people who consume fish from the Great Lakes at least weekly may face excess cancer risks, even if the fish is contaminated at just one-third to one-fifth of the FDA-set legal limit for the pesticides DDT and dieldrin.[20] The National Academy of Sciences (NAS) concluded that many limits were based "on reasoning that was questionable at the time and has been rendered obsolete."[21]

➤ The FDA has set maximum contamination levels for only about a dozen of the hundreds of contaminants that scientists have identified in fish. Only one, for PCBs, has a formal regulatory limit that is legally enforceable.

➤ The FDA samples only a small fraction of commercial seafood for possible chemical or bacterial contamination—representing less than 1 percent of domestic seafood, and 3 percent of imported seafood.[22] The NAS concluded that the available data used to assess risks, warn consumers, and set priorities are "grossly inadequate."[23]

It's up to the states to protect consumers who eat fish that aren't transported across state lines. This includes fish sold locally or fish caught for sport—or for that day's meal. The main way that states alert people about potential risks of contaminated fish is through "fish consumption advisories." These are disseminated through media announcements, printed brochures, posted notices in public places, or information in fishing license applications. Generally, a state considers issuing an advisory when the contaminant levels found in fish exceed levels set by the federal government. But, as we've just pointed out, the federal levels themselves often do not adequately protect consumers. And there are widespread inconsistencies in standards used by states to issue advisories. Budgetary constraints often limit a state's ability to sample, monitor for, and publicize potential contamination—and all too often people ignore advisories anyway.

Prodded first by Public Voice for Food and Health Policy, a Washington-based consumer group, Congress has been considering ways to strengthen fish safety laws. In 1990 Congress was on the brink of passing a law, when disputes arose as to whether the FDA or the USDA should be in charge of fish inspection. Given USDA's dismal record in inspecting meat, many groups favor the FDA. As this book went to press, Congress was reconsidering both approaches, while the FDA was improving its existing fish inspection program.

SAFE FOOD CHOICES

◆ Eat a variety of seafood to lessen potential contamination from any single source. If you are pregnant or thinking of becoming pregnant, or if you're nursing, be particularly careful to avoid fish likely to be contaminated, such as swordfish and bluefish.

◆ If you catch your own fish, make sure the waters are approved for fishing or for harvesting shellfish. Find out about any fish advisories issued for your area. If you're uncertain, check with your state or local health or environmental protection department.

◆ Avoid eating raw shellfish. If you do choose to eat raw shellfish, exercise extreme caution. Be sure that it hasn't been harvested from waters closed to shellfishing (ask to see the certified shipper's tag that must accompany shellfish products). People with weakened immune systems shouldn't eat raw seafood at all.

◆ If you eat sushi and sashimi, be aware that you're taking a slight risk. Eat it only at reputable restaurants where you can feel confident that proper precautions are taken. And be especially careful with the types of fish that are most likely to be contaminated with bacteria, raw Pacific salmon and Pacific rockfish (red snapper). Also be careful with dishes such as ceviche, in which fish is "cooked" by marinating in lime juice—marinating probably won't kill bacteria or parasites.

◆ Shrimp is sometimes treated with sulfites right on board fishing vessels to prevent "black spot." Unfortunately, sulfites may not be listed on labels. So if you are sulfite sensitive (see page 166), avoid shrimp.

AT THE MARKET

◆ Buy your fish and shellfish from reputable dealers with proper storage and handling facilities. You're taking a chance if you buy from roadside sellers. Ask your fish-market manager about the source of fish or seafood for sale. If it was caught near urban coastal areas or in waters you think may be polluted, don't buy it.

◆ Choose fish that are the least likely to be contaminated. In general, choose younger, smaller fish; they've had less time to accumulate toxins from surrounding water or other fish.

Choosing the safest fish

You may be able to reduce your exposure to chemical contaminants in fish if you keep in mind two general guidelines: 1) offshore fish are less likely to be contaminated than near-shore or freshwater fish, and 2) within each of these three groups, the fattier the fish, the more likely it is to be contaminated. A few exceptions to these rules include bluefish and striped bass, which tend to be much more contaminated than coastal salmon. (Salmon from the Great Lakes is riskier.)

The following chart lists some of the most popular fish, according to whether they are freshwater, near-shore, or offshore varieties, and in order according to fat content. The safest bets are the fish in the upper left corner—note the exceptions, though.

OFFSHORE	NEAR-SHORE	FRESHWATER
cod	✗ striped bass	yellow perch
haddock	✓ pink salmon	freshwater bass
pollock	✗ bluefish	white perch
yellowfin tuna	✓ chum salmon	brook trout
flounder, sole	✓ sockeye salmon	rainbow trout
ocean perch	sardines	✗ catfish
✗ swordfish	herring	✗ carp
Pacific halibut		lake whitefish
albacore tuna		lake trout

✗ These species probably have high levels of contaminants. **Swordfish** frequently exceed allowable levels of methyl mercury. Migratory fish such as **striped bass** and **bluefish** are frequently tainted with PCBs, even if they're caught offshore. **Catfish** and **carp** are bottom feeders, and are particularly vulnerable to contamination from tainted sediments. Most commercially harvested catfish is farm-raised, and relatively uncontaminated with pesticides, but drug residues from aquaculture might be a problem.

✓ Despite their high fat content, **salmon** (except those caught from the Great Lakes) tend to be relatively free of chemical contaminants.

◆ Don't buy ready-to-eat seafood that's displayed right next to raw seafood, since it can be contaminated with bacteria from the raw seafood.

IN YOUR KITCHEN

◆ Handle and store raw seafood carefully so that it doesn't come into contact with cooked food. Keep all seafood chilled in the coldest part of the refrigerator, and use it within one day. Many refrigerator freezers aren't as cold as 0 degrees, so don't store frozen fish there too long. Thaw frozen seafood in the refrigerator or microwave, not on the counter, and then cook it promptly.

◆ Store live shellfish—such as clams, mussels, and oysters—in well-ventilated containers, not in air tight plastic bags or boxes. Live lobsters and crabs should also be in well-ventilated containers with damp paper towels over them in the refrigerator. Don't use any shellfish that have died during storage.

◆ Carefully clean and rinse your work space, knives, containers, and hands before and after preparing seafood. Use a plastic or other nonporous cutting board when you handle fish, since it will be easier to clean well.

◆ Keep in mind that industrial chemicals such as PCBs can accumulate in the fatty portions of fish such as bluefish. To minimize your exposure to these chemicals, remove all the skin and cut away the belly flap and any darker meat along the top or the center of the fillet. Avoid sauces made from liquid fish drippings or cooking water, and avoid stews and soups that call for whole fish with internal organs, since toxins can accumulate there. Don't eat the green-colored "tomalley" (the hepatopancreas) in lobster or the "mustard" in blue crab, which can concentrate PCBs, cadmium, and other chemicals to very high levels.

◆ Cook fish completely—in general, about 6 to 10 minutes per inch of thickness. Fish must be heated to a core temperature of 140 to 145 degrees for five minutes to kill parasites. Your best bets are broiling, baking, or poaching. When you barbecue, bake, or broil fish, use a rack to allow oils to drain from the fish while cooking. Avoid deep frying and pan frying, since these methods seal in natural oils and add extra fat and calories. (For grilled fish, follow the steps in "Grilling safely to avoid natural carcinogens," page 112.) Check fish occasionally for doneness—it's cooked when it turns from translucent to opaque or white, and is firm but still moist. If you cook fish in your microwave, cover it and cook it thoroughly.

◆ If fish smells rotten, throw it away!

◆ If you want to be sure to kill microorganisms, when you cook large whole crabs, boil them for at least 8 minutes, or steam them for more than 25 minutes. And steam oysters, clams, and mussels for four to six minutes.

WHAT YOU CAN DO AS A CITIZEN

◆ Demand that Congress require that the FDA establish an effective federal seafood-safety program. The program should include better control and cleanup of water pollution; adequate inspection and testing of fish for natural toxins and microbiological and chemical contaminants; protection for whistleblowers; and controls on aquaculture.

◆ Until shellfish are certified as safe, ask the FDA to require notices on packages of molluscan shellfish and signs at fish markets and restaurants that serve raw shellfish: "Warning: Eating raw oysters, mussels, or clams may cause serious illness or death, particularly in people who have liver disease, cancer, or other chronic illnesses that weaken the immune system. If you eat raw shellfish and become sick, seek immediate medical attention."

CHAPTER 6
WHAT'S SAFE
TO DRINK?

WHAT'S SAFE
TO DRINK?

You've been out working in your garden on a hot summer day—and you're thirsty. You head for the fridge—there's a six-pack of beer, a bottle of club soda, some soft drinks, and a couple of fruit drinks. On the top shelf is a carton of milk and a bottle of orange juice, and on the refrigerator door, some wine coolers. And over there, just a few feet from the refrigerator, is your kitchen faucet with all the tap water you can drink.

What's the safest thirst quencher? Let's look at your choices.

DRINKING WATER

In fact, water may be one of your safest choices...if yours happens to be safe. For most people it is—particularly for those people served by large municipal water systems. But consider:

➤ In 1988 more than 11 million people drank tap water that contained illegal levels of contaminants. That same year, one of every four public water systems that operated year-round violated federal drinking water laws.

➤ More than 700 contaminants have been found in public drinking water—including pesticides, solvents, metals, radon, and harmful microbes. Unfortunately, the EPA has set legal limits, or "maximum contaminant levels" (MCLs), for just 54 of the 700-plus contaminants. Still, these 54 include some particularly nasty chemicals, such as the carcinogens arsenic and benzene.

To find out what's in your municipal water, start by asking your utility for its latest water analysis. This system isn't foolproof, though. The General Accounting Office recently found evidence that some (unnamed) utilities falsify test results. Even so, looking at those results is the only way—short of spending hundreds of dollars to test your tap water—to know what contaminants might be there. Your utility is required to provide the information to you free of charge. If you don't know whom to call, the EPA Safe Drinking Water Hotline—1-800-426-4791 or (202) 382-5533 in Alaska and Washington, D.C.—can tell you.

The EPA will also send you a free booklet, "Is Your Drinking Water Safe?" You can use this booklet to compare your utility's water-testing results with the legal limits. If your water exceeds any of the MCLs or isn't being tested for some of them, your utility is probably breaking the law, and you should call your state water supply agency to find out what's being done to correct the problem. And if you need to filter your water, they will be able to help you choose the right filter to do the job.

There are three particular instances when you may want to have your tap water tested to be sure it's safe: if you suspect the presence of lead; if your water comes from a private well; or if your utility serves fewer than 3,300 people (a "small" system, according to the EPA, which means it has to test for fewer contaminants and is more likely to have violations). Use only independent, state-certified laboratories for testing—the EPA Safe Drinking Water Hotline can help you find an approved lab in your state.

Lead, which attacks the nervous system and causes mental impairment, is a leading health hazard for American children. You can't rely on the results of your water utility's testing to tell you if there's lead in your water, since their analysis only reflects the quality of the water when it leaves the public treatment plant. By the time it comes out of your tap, your water may have picked up lead from the plumbing.

Lead-contaminated drinking water is most often a

Cavities, cancer, and the fluoride controversy

Since 1945 when fluoride was first added to water, a battle has raged over its benefits and risks. The dental establishment maintains that fluoride helps prevent tooth decay. Opponents charge that fluoridation represents involuntary medication and causes cancer and other diseases.

The battle erupted anew in 1990 when a government-sponsored study of fluoride reported bone cancer in five male rats. No bone cancers occurred in female rats or mice. The only other high-quality cancer study was conducted by Procter & Gamble, which found benign bone tumors in mice, but none in rats. More extensive studies should be conducted immediately to verify—or refute—these results.

Several studies have found no association between water fluoridation and cancer in humans, which is comforting. However, those studies could only have detected major increases in cancer, not modest ones.

If fluoride is a carcinogen at all, it is a very weak one. But even weak carcinogens shouldn't be added to the food or water supply. If fluoride is confirmed to promote cancer, safer methods—such as the use of dentifrices—must be adopted to protect growing teeth.

Cancer aside, if children get too much fluoride, they can get dental fluorosis, or mottled and discolored teeth. According to the EPA, assuming average dietary levels of fluoride, up to 1 ppm in water won't cause dental fluorosis.

Be sure your children are getting enough fluoride, but not too much. Find out how much fluoride is in your tap water (see page 132) or bottled water (ask the manufacturer). Teach your children to rinse thoroughly after brushing their teeth, and not to swallow toothpaste. And urge the EPA to lower the current legal limit of 4 ppm fluoride in drinking water to no greater than 1 ppm.

problem in houses or buildings that are either very old or very new. Plumbing installed before 1930—either interior plumbing or the connection that joins you to your public water supply—is most likely to contain lead.

In addition, the use of lead solder with copper pipes is widespread. In that case, the newer the home, the greater the risk of lead contamination. As time passes, mineral deposits form a coating on the inside of the pipes. But during the first five years, before the coating forms, water is in direct contact with the lead. What's more, even your faucet can contribute lead to your drinking water. Most faucets are made of chrome-plated brass, and brass contains anywhere from 3 to 8 percent lead.

Since even very low levels of lead are extremely dangerous for children and fetuses, it's a good idea to test your water for lead if you have a child, or if you're pregnant or thinking of becoming pregnant. While waiting for the test results, take these precautions: before drinking water from a faucet that hasn't been used for six hours or longer, flush out the cold-water pipes by running the water until it becomes as cold as it will get. This could take anywhere from five seconds to two minutes or longer. You don't have to waste the water—save it for cleaning, watering houseplants, or other uses.

Fill your kettle and drinking water containers with cold water in the evening after washing the dishes, since by then any lead will have flushed out of the pipes. And since hot water is likely to contain higher levels of lead, use only cold water from the cold-water tap for drinking, cooking, and especially for making baby formula.

Private well water and **water from small utilities** isn't tested by the government or is inadequately tested—so testing is up to you. Consider testing your water for organic chemicals if you live near a hazardous waste dump, industrial park, chemical plant, or military base. If you live in an agricultural area or near a livestock facility,

Treat it right: water filters

Before you join the 5 million people who own or rent water-treatment units, consider this: You can't fix your water until you know what's wrong with it. If you don't get the right unit for the job or don't maintain it properly, you could be wasting your money or even be making your water worse:

➤ One man who was on kidney dialysis and required a sodium-free diet spent more than $2,000 for a water softener after the salesman assured him it wouldn't put more sodium into his water. He had the water tested, and discovered that the unit was tripling the sodium content.

➤ An elderly couple on a fixed income spent $1,000 for a unit to remove the pesticide DBCP. But they didn't know how (or couldn't afford) to maintain it properly. The filter wore out and stopped removing the pesticide from their water.

➤ A pregnant woman was warned by her doctor that the nitrate in her well water could be dangerous to her baby. She bought an activated-carbon filter, which doesn't remove nitrates effectively. Luckily, she contacted her county health department and they helped her find the right unit to do the job.

The lesson? Know what problem you're trying to fix; if you suspect that your water is contaminated, have it tested by a certified lab (see page 132). Don't fall for sales scams—be especially wary of in-home water tests conducted by water-filter salespeople. And don't think that an "EPA-approved" label means you'll be protected. (Any filter that uses silver has to be registered by the EPA—no federal agency approves water-treatment units.)

Since an effective water filter can cost anywhere from $100 to thousands of dollars, do some research before you buy one. Several excellent guides to water-safety problems and filters are described on page 207. Here's a quick look at the different types of filters and what they can do:

CONTAMINANTS:	INORGANIC	MICROBIAL	ORGANIC	RADIOACTIVE
TREATMENT TECHNIQUES:				
carbon adsorption	★	★	★★★★	★★
distillation	★★★	★★	★★	
reverse osmosis	★★★	★ ★	★★	★★
water softener	★			★★

The more stars, the more effectively the treatment technique removes that type of contaminant. No star means the treatment technique does not remove that type of contaminant.

Inorganic contaminants include the metals lead and mercury (which damage the nervous system), and nitrates (which cause "blue-baby" syndrome). Valuable minerals such as iron and zinc, which most of us don't get enough of, are also removed.

Microbial contaminants include *Giardia*, viruses, and coliform or other bacteria.

Organic contaminants include pesticides, solvents such as trichloroethylene, and many other chemicals. Some cause cancer or harm the liver, kidney, or nervous system. Some organic chemicals in tap water are volatile, which means they vaporize easily and can be inhaled when you take a shower.

Radioactive contaminants include radium and radon, which may cause cancer. Radon removal may require a shielded water-treatment unit or removal outside the house.

have the water tested for nitrate, bacteria, and pesticides. Though nitrate poisonings are rare, they still occur. For instance, in June 1986, 2-month-old Lacy Jo Geyer died of nitrate poisoning in South Dakota. The rural well water which her mother used to prepare formula contained three times as much nitrate as the EPA and the World Health Organization consider safe for infants. Twenty to 25 percent of the private wells tested in some agricultural states have exceeded the EPA's health standards for nitrates.[1] You may be able to get your water tested for nitrate for $10 or $15; tests for a range of pesticides may cost hundreds of dollars. In addition, have it tested periodically for bacteria and inorganic compounds.

What do you do if testing finds that your tap water is contaminated? Home filters can help, but only if you choose the right one for addressing your problem, and if you maintain it properly. If you don't, you're throwing money down the drain. (See "Treat it right: water filters" page 136, and page 207 for some excellent resources.)

IS BOTTLED BETTER?

Almost one out of every 15 households nationwide—and one out of every three households in California—consumes bottled water as their primary source of drinking water. The industry has grown approximately 400 percent over the last decade. Bottled water costs 500 to 1,000 times as much as public water. But does all that extra money buy you a safer product? Don't count on it. At the present time, bottled water is regulated even less than tap water (and a lot of bottled water actually comes from tap water).

In 1987, a state survey in Massachusetts found that 13 of 15 brands of bottled water exceeded one or more federal or state guidelines for pollutants.[2] That same year, a New York survey found traces of toluene, carbon tetrachloride, and other solvents in 48 out of 93 bottled-water samples.[3] And in an infamous 1990 incident, bottles of Perrier were found to be contaminated with trace levels of benzene, a carcinogen. The benzene was apparently naturally occurring in the gas used to put the fizz into Perrier, but the usual filtration system used to remove the benzene wasn't working properly. The water was taken off the market until the bottler fixed the problem. (Speaking of naturally occurring ingredients, some mineral water contains high levels of arsenic.[4] Others have high sodium levels, so be careful with these if you are on a sodium-restricted diet.)

One way to check on the safety of your favorite brand of bottled water is to write to the bottler and ask for the latest tests on all the chemicals it tests for, and then compare those results with the EPA guidelines or standards.

WHAT YOU CAN DO AS A CITIZEN

While you're writing letters, you might want to write some to your congressional representatives and to your local water utility. Ask your congressional representatives to:

◆ Ensure the safety of bottled water. Require bottled water to meet the same health standards as tap water, and require monitoring to ensure that the standards are met. Set up a procedure for notifying the public if a bottled water is found to violate drinking-water standards. Require a comprehensive study to determine whether processing and storage contribute to contamination of bottled water. And require labeling that tells the original source of the water; the type of water; the type of treatment, if any; and the sodium and fluoride content.

◆ Clamp down on misleading advertising about the safety of bottled water, and prohibit misleading home water tests and other water treatment sales scams. Require federal government certification of all home water treatment units.

◆ Impose stiffer penalties on public water utilities that fail to notify the public when drinking water violates health standards, or that falsify information provided to the federal government or the public about contaminants.

If your local water supply is contaminated with organic chemicals, ask your utility to:

◆ Install an activated carbon filter system at the treatment plant. In Cincinnati, the first city to install such a system, this extra protection costs the average family just six cents more a day.

ALCOHOLIC BEVERAGES

If you're looking for safety first, don't choose alcohol. Not only does alcohol impair driving and coordination, it can also cause chronic diseases—including liver cirrhosis, cancer, and high blood pressure. In heavy drinkers, alcohol can cause heart or brain damage. All told, alcohol is responsible for more than 105,000 deaths a year.[5] It contributes to about half of all homicides. Alcohol-related traffic fatalities are the leading killer of young people.[6]

Don't drink at all if you're pregnant or trying to get pregnant, and never give alcoholic beverages to children or adolescents. Stay away from alcohol if you might be driving or engaging in activities that require a high level of attention or skills—just one or two drinks can impair those abilities for up to five hours.

Alcoholism seems to run in families. If there's alcoholism in yours, you may wish to avoid alcohol altogether. People who both smoke and drink have greatly increased risks of cancers of the mouth, throat, larynx, and esophagus. (The International Agency for Research on Cancer has classified alcoholic beverages as a known human carcinogen.) And don't drink alcohol if you're using other drugs—legal or illegal. Other drugs can worsen the effects of alcohol, while the alcohol can decrease the effectiveness of medications. Even aspirin and alcohol may be a bad mix, since aspirin may interfere with the stomach's ability to break down alcohol.[7]

If you do choose to drink alcohol, confine your drinking to "low-risk" levels—no more than one drink a day if you're a woman, or two drinks a day if you're a man.[8] One drink means one can (12 ounces) of beer, one glass (5 ounces) of wine, or one mixed drink (one and a half ounces of distilled spirits).

Crystal-clear lead warning

After listening to a talk by fellow Columbia University professor Joseph Graziano on the dangers of lead, Conrad Blum, a soon-to-be father, decided to use a home lead-testing kit on some of his family's ceramic dishes. "For fun," he also tested a lead-crystal wine glass. It came out positive. That's when Blum and Graziano decided to test crystal decanters and goblets in the laboratory. Among their findings:[9]

➤ The lead content of port wines that were stored in crystal decanters for four months jumped from 89 parts per billion (ppb) to between 2,162 and 5,331 ppb. (The EPA's current maximum level for lead in drinking water is 50 ppb, although they will probably lower it.)

➤ On average, lead levels doubled (33 ppb to 68 ppb) in white wine that had sat in lead-crystal goblets for just an hour.

Lead will leach from crystal into any liquid, not just alcohol. Lead can damage kidneys and cause nervous-system disorders. It's particularly dangerous for children and pregnant women.

Your best bets: The FDA has warned people not to use lead crystal every day, and not to store food or beverages in it. Women of child-bearing age shouldn't use lead crystal at all. Waterford has stopped making lead-crystal baby bottles, but if you have one or are given one, never use it for feeding your baby.

The largest risks in alcoholic beverages come from the alcohol itself. However, other risks may lurk in your favorite drink:

➤ **Urethane.** Many wines and distilled spirits (rarely beer) are tainted with tiny amounts of a powerful cancer-causing chemical, urethane.[10] Urethane isn't added intentionally, but forms naturally during fermentation, distillation, or storage. If you drink contaminated products only occasionally, the urethane levels probably aren't high enough to worry about. But if you're a regular drinker (particularly if your favorite brand happens to be highly contaminated), the urethane may pose a serious risk. The most contaminated products, which have been outlawed in Canada but not the United States, are fruit brandies. The FDA has accepted voluntary standards proposed by distillers and wine makers, but purer liquors and wines still may not be available until the year 2000. And for table wines and dessert wines, the limits on urethane don't necessarily represent any safety improvement.

➤ **Sulfites.** Sulfites occur both naturally and as an additive in virtually all wines. Vintners have used sulfites for hundreds of years to prevent the growth of bacteria and yeasts that can turn wine into vinegar. Sulfites also serve as preservatives to inhibit spoilage during months and years of storage. Although sulfites aren't a problem for everyone, they are for many asthmatics (and some non-asthmatics), who can experience severe allergic reactions to them (see page 166). Because of this problem, all wines bottled after mid-1987 have to bear labels saying "contains sulfites" if they contain more than 10 parts per

---

Wine-cooler facts

If you believed the ads for wine coolers, you might think they were low-calorie health drinks. Instead, they are often sugar-laden beverages that contain more calories than other forms of alcohol. And wine coolers contain more alcohol than beer does—6 percent alcohol (by volume), compared to 4 or 5 percent in beer.

million of sulfites—and most wines do. Organic wines are not necessarily sulfite-free. But since organic wines are produced without synthetic pesticides and fertilizers, they are certainly kinder to the environment and farm workers. Brewers dropped the use of sulfite preservatives rather than having to list them on their beer labels.

Beer, wine, and liquor companies spend more than $2 billion each year advertising and promoting alcoholic beverages. Slick advertising associates alcohol with health, good times and friends, celebrations, and personal success. In a 1988 CSPI survey of 180 children 7 to 12 years old, the average child could name more alcoholic beverages than U.S. presidents.[11] Other surveys find that the average age at which young people begin drinking is 13. By the time they are in college, students consume an average of 34 gallons of alcoholic beverages per year—including 30 gallons of beer.[12]

There aren't any quick fixes for the problems created by beer, wine, and liquor. But consumers are starting to get a little more information about the health risks. All alcoholic beverages produced after November 1989 have to carry a warning message about the dangers of drinking during pregnancy and drinking before driving. Some states and municipalities now require warning posters wherever alcoholic beverages are sold.

WHAT YOU CAN DO AS A CITIZEN

Here are some important steps that the government can take to prevent alcohol problems. If you are concerned about this issue, write to your senators and congressional representatives, and to state and local elected officials, to demand the following changes:

◆ **Require health and safety information about alcohol.** A variety of health and safety facts should be provided on all alcoholic-beverage containers (just as is required for cigarettes), in all advertising and promotional materials, and wherever alcoholic beverages are sold. Such notices should address the risks of drinking while taking other drugs, the increased risks of liver disease and cancer, and the danger of drinking during pregnancy. Labels should also indicate that alcohol can be addictive and that it is illegal to purchase alcohol if you're under the age of 21. The law should also require that full ingredient and calorie listings be printed on all alcoholic-beverage containers, as well as a toll-free number that consumers could call for information about alcoholism treatment. And television and radio advertisements should be balanced with an equal number of messages highlighting the risks associated with drinking.

◆ **Clean up alcohol advertising practices.** Eliminate alcoholic-beverage marketing, such as on college campuses, that is aimed at people under the legal drinking age. Prohibit alcohol advertisements that depict high-risk activities, use celebrities and rock stars, and glamorize drinking. Halt alcohol advertising on billboards in residential areas, where children can see them every day.

OTHER BEVERAGE CHOICES

➤ **Soft drinks.** Devoid of nutritional value, soft drinks contain heavy doses of sugar and calories (or artificial sweeteners), plus artificial colorings, artificial flavorings, and sometimes caffeine—most of which are additives to avoid (see Chapter 7). Unfortunately, Americans consume huge amounts of soft drinks—more than 30 gallons per person per year. Soft drinks have edged out milk as the nation's most popular drink.

➤ **Coffee, tea.** Caffeine isn't a problem for everyone, but some people should avoid it—including pregnant women and children (see Chapter 7). Some decaffeinated coffees may contain tiny amounts of a decaffeinating agent, methylene chloride. Methylene chloride has caused cancer in animal studies and should not be used, but the amounts remaining in hot coffee are trivial and not worth worrying about. (Many producers use another agent, ethyl acetate, which is safe.)

Some people wonder how much caffeine is left in decaffeinated coffee, which is usually advertised as "97 percent caffeine-free." Does the coffee still contain 3 percent caffeine, or is 97 percent of the caffeine removed? Well, rest easy—the second choice is correct. Almost all the caffeine is removed during the decaffeination process.

One recent study indicated that decaffeinated coffee may raise blood cholesterol levels.[13] Although that problem deserves further study, switching back to regular coffee may not be the best solution. Numerous studies over the past 30 years have either linked coffee to, or exonerated it from, a higher risk of heart disease. The mixed results may reflect a small but real effect that shows up in some studies but not others. If you have had a heart attack or some form of heart disease, it would make sense to consume little or no coffee, either regular or decaffeinated.

You could bypass the coffee controversies altogether by switching to herbal teas. Just make sure the teas don't contain coltsfoot, sassafras, or comfrey, which are suspected carcinogens. Sassafras was banned from food in 1960 because of cancer concerns.

If you drink lots of regular, nonherbal tea, one concern besides caffeine is tannin, a naturally occurring mixture of chemicals that may be cancer-causing. Your best bet is to drink your tea the British way—with milk, which binds the tannin and makes it insoluble.

But if you drink a lot of coffee or tea and add whole milk or cream to it, you could also be adding plenty of calories and saturated fat to your diet. Skim milk is your best bet. Don't use nondairy coffee whiteners. Some

And for baby?

What babies eat during their first six months of life is critical to their development. And of course, most babies don't eat at all during that time—they drink. Breast milk is best, since formulas don't quite duplicate the food that Nature designed for your baby. For example, recent evidence indicates that formulas are missing omega-3 fatty acids, which may be important for optimal eye and brain development.[14]

If you rely on infant formulas for half or more of your baby's nourishment, check the ingredient label, and buy a formula that contains soy (or soybean) oil, a good source of omega-3 fatty acids. Liquid formulas are usually made with soybean oil; powdered formulas may or may not contain it. Don't try to supply omega-3 fatty acids by giving your baby fish oil—infants have trouble absorbing fish oil that is not commercially mixed with milk.

Breast milk is almost a "perfect" food, but, tragically, it may be contaminated with PCBs and other pollutants. Ellen Silbergeld, Ph.D., a toxicologist at the University of Maryland, says that this contamination is "a signal that our society should not ignore. It's an outrage."

Still, most experts agree with the World Health Organization that the unique advantages of breast-feeding outweigh the risks.[15]

Silbergeld suggests that if you have had "unusual" exposures to contaminants on the job or by accident, you should consider having your breast milk tested. Call your state health department or a university toxicology department for details. "Some women who have high levels of contaminants in their milk may opt to breast-feed for a shorter time than they would otherwise," notes Silbergeld.

brands are made with saturated vegetable fats, such as coconut and palm oils, and all will add fat and calories.

If you use a sweetener, you may be better off using sugar or honey than an artificial sweetener, unless you're diabetic. There are fewer than 25 calories in a teaspoon of either sugar or honey.

And what should you drink your tea or coffee from? Styrofoam cups won't hurt you, even if you drink your tea with lemon—but they certainly aren't good for the environment. A mug is better. Since you'll probably be drinking from your favorite mug or cup every day, though, it's best to avoid using an antique cup or imported pottery, since they may leach lead into your beverage. (See "Unleaded, please," page 176).

➤ **Milk.** Milk is a great choice, as long as you buy skim (liquid or powdered) or 1 percent low-fat—and as long as you don't have allergies to milk or lactose intolerance. The safety concerns with milk aren't serious enough for you to avoid it, and it packs in essential nutrients, including calcium, protein, and riboflavin.

➤ **Fruit juice.** This is another good choice, and a particularly tasty one when you squeeze it yourself. Most pure fruit juices are high in vitamins A and C and contain modest amounts of other vitamins. They don't contain anywhere near the fiber that fruit itself has, but then, you can't drink fruit. Just don't confuse fruit juice with fruit drinks—the latter might not contain any real juice to speak of. They might be fortified with vitamins, but they're still full of sugar or artificial sweeteners and may be as expensive as real juice.

CHAPTER 7

THE TRUTH ABOUT ADDITIVES

THE TRUTH ABOUT ADDITIVES

If you and your family never, ever eat processed foods, then you can probably skip this chapter. But if you're like most Americans, and sometimes find yourself eating food with ingredients you can't even pronounce, much less pronounce with certainty that they're safe—read on.

The average American consumes about five pounds of food additives per year. If you include sugar and salt, that figure is closer to 115 pounds. The good news is that the vast majority of the hundreds of chemicals that are added to our food are safe. The bad news is that some of them are not, but still haven't been banned from the food supply. And the other news is that some additives haven't been tested enough to determine whether they're safe or not.

WHAT DO THOSE ADDITIVES DO, ANYWAY?

Cooks were using additives in food long before General Foods and Coca-Cola set up their prolific chemistry labs. Brine and smoke preservatives, seaweed and starch thickeners, herb and spice flavorings, plant extract colorings, and flavor enhancers made from dried fish have all been used for ages. It's just that today Nature has been replaced by products from laboratories. Chemical additives are used for various technical purposes:

➤ **Antioxidants** are added to oil-containing foods to prevent the oil from going rancid.

➤ **Chelating agents** trap trace amounts of metal atoms that would otherwise cause food to discolor or go rancid.

➤ **Emulsifiers** keep oil and water mixed together.

➤ **Flavor enhancers** have little or no flavor of their own, but are used to accentuate the natural flavor of foods.

➤ **Thickening agents** absorb some of the water present in food, making the food thicker. They also keep oils, water, and solids well mixed.

In short, additives permit longer shelf lives, cheaper ingredient costs, more food products, and higher profits for chemical and food manufacturers.

The chart on pages 158–159 lists dozens of additives commonly found in our food, and indicates whether they are safe, whether you should avoid them, or whether they need better testing. Here's more detailed information on the ones to avoid, and why. Keep in mind as you read this section that fat, cholesterol, and sodium generally pose greater health risks than these additives do (see our discussion of nutrition in Chapter 1). At the most, additives may contribute to several hundred or thousand deaths a year. But fat, sodium, and cholesterol excesses—and fiber deficiencies—contribute to hundreds of thousands.

TOP 10 ADDITIVES TO SUBTRACT FROM YOUR DIET

No single food additive poses a severe danger to the entire population. However, several additives pose small risks to the general public and great risks to individuals who are sensitive or allergic to them. Ideally, the additives that pose any risk at all to any portion of the public would be phased out of the food supply and replaced by entirely safe substances.

Children's foods, in particular, should be as free as possible from questionable additives. It simply doesn't make sense to expose children to chemicals that might add even the slightest risk to their future health. Unfortunately, foods targeted specifically to children—

Additives and hyperactive kids

Can additives add up to hyperactive children? For some children, the answer is yes.

Twenty years ago, California allergist Ben Feingold, M.D., hit the headlines and talk shows with claims that food additives and certain natural substances in food were the culprits behind a large fraction of hyperactivity. Over the years, numerous studies were undertaken to investigate the problem. Most of the studies were limited to only a few additives, such as colorings. Others were flawed because they used inappropriately low doses of additives.

In one of the first definitive studies, researchers at the University of California, Berkeley, found that out of 22 hyperactive subjects, 2 children reacted adversely to a mixture of artificial colorings, one dramatically.[1] This study provided evidence that Feingold's theory was correct, though his estimate of the extent of the problem was overstated.

One 1989 study looked at children's behavior after making several dietary changes.[2] The study involved 24 hyperactive boys between the ages of three-and-a-half and six. All had sleep problems or physical symptoms, such as stuffy noses or stomachaches, that might reflect food sensitivities. In the study, the children were fed specially prepared low-sugar, vitamin-rich diets that eliminated colorings, flavorings, MSG, caffeine, preservatives, chocolate, and other substances (such as milk) that parents reported might affect their child. After four weeks on the diet, 10 of the boys showed an average of 45 percent improvement in behavior, four showed a more modest improvement, and 10 exhibited no effect, according to their parents' reports.

If your child is hyperactive and you suspect that additives might be the cause, try removing foods containing them from your child's diet (there are other good reasons to do so, anyway).[3] The Feingold Association (see page 209) can provide information on how. Don't hope for miracles, however. The researchers in the 1989 study noted that "not a single parent believed that participation in this study had transformed their child into an easy-to-manage person."

candies, soft drinks, cupcakes, ice pops, and sugary break-fast cereals—contain many questionable additives. The following 10 additives, listed alphabetically, appear to pose the biggest risks to some or all consumers.

ACESULFAME K

Acesulfame K, sold commercially as Sunette or Sweet One, was approved by the FDA in 1988 as a sugar substitute in packet or tablet form, in chewing gum, dry mixes for beverages, instant coffee and tea, gelatin desserts, puddings, and nondairy creamers. The manufacturer has asked the FDA to approve acesulfame K for soft drinks and baked goods.

The public is waiting for an artificial sweetener that is unquestionably safe. But this one isn't it. Even compared to aspartame and saccharin (which are afflicted with their own safety problems—see below), acesulfame K is the worst. The additive is inadequately tested—the FDA based its approval on tests of acesulfame K that fell short of the FDA's own standards. But even those tests indicate that the additive causes cancer in animals, which means it may increase cancer risk in humans. In 1987, CSPI urged the FDA not to approve acesulfame K, but was ignored. After the FDA gave the chemical its blessing, CSPI urged that it be banned. The FDA hasn't yet ruled on that request.

◆ **Safe Food choice:** Avoid acesulfame K and products containing it. Your sweet tooth isn't worth it.

ARTIFICIAL COLORINGS

Food manufacturers frequently use artificial colorings, often in combination with artificial flavorings, to replace natural ingredients. The red or yellow color of a soft drink is rarely due to natural cherry or orange extract. Artificial colorings are much cheaper than real, natural ingredients. The artificial substances are also usually more stable.

Artificial colorings may be either naturally derived or synthetic. The naturally derived colorants, such as beta-carotene (the vegetable form of vitamin A used to color margarine), beet-juice extract, or substances extracted from flower petals, haven't generally been well tested, but they're presumed to be safe. The great bulk of artificial colorings used in food are synthetic dyes: Blue No. 1, Blue No. 2, Citrus Red No. 2, Green No. 3, Red No. 3, Red No. 40, Yellow No. 5, and Yellow No. 6.

Too much iodine?

Goiter, a disfiguring disease in which the thyroid gland is greatly enlarged, was once a severe problem in parts of the country in which soil contained little iodine. Public-health experts advised adding a little iodine (e.g., potassium iodide) to table salt to ensure that people would get an extra dose of it every time they salted their food. That strategy quickly erased the "goiter belt" from U.S. maps.

But health experts may have succeeded more than they had hoped. Now we get iodine not just from table salt, but from a multitude of processed foods that contain iodized salt, and foods that are contaminated with iodine used as an antiseptic. Because iodine has proliferated to such an extent, goiter caused by iodine excess could be a problem.

The FDA has found amounts of iodine that greatly exceed the recommended daily intake in some processed foods. In 1991, the FDA stopped a company called C. R. Eggs, Inc., from selling eggs that contained too much iodine. (The company claimed that the eggs could lower cholesterol.) The FDA ought to crack down on other companies that expose Americans to too much iodine.

Combinations of these dyes yield the rainbow of colors found in breakfast cereals, candies, ice cream, soft drinks, and frostings.

For decades, synthetic food dyes have been suspected of being toxic or carcinogenic, and many have been banned. Safety questions surround the few that remain. Take Yellow No. 5, for example. America's second-most-popular food color (after Red No. 40), it is associated with allergic reactions in some people, including hives, runny or stuffy noses, and occasionally severe breathing difficulties. The FDA has estimated that between 47,000 and 94,000 Americans are sensitive to Yellow No. 5. (For some reason, most of the people who have been found to be sensitive to the dye are also sensitive to aspirin.)

Red No. 3 has been banned for some purposes, because it caused thyroid tumors in male rats. The FDA says it plans to propose that other uses be banned, but meanwhile, in 1990 more than 180,000 pounds were approved for use in our food. Several other artificial colorings, including Blue No. 2 and Red No. 40, need to be better tested to determine whether or not they promote cancer.

Currently, only Yellow No. 5 must be individually listed on ingredient labels; other artificial dyes are listed simply as "artificial colorings" (but that will change when new FDA rules go into effect in 1993).

◆ **Safe Food choice:** Whenever possible, choose foods without dyes. They're mostly used in foods of questionable nutritional worth anyway. Natural ingredients should provide all the color your food needs.

ASPARTAME

This sugar substitute, sold commercially as Equal and NutraSweet, was hailed as the savior of dieters who for decades had put up with saccharin's unpleasant aftertaste. Proponents touted it as the closest you could come to sugar without the calories. Discovered in 1965, aspartame was approved for limited use in 1981. In 1983, the FDA approved its use in soft drinks.

But as loudly as it was hailed by the industry, aspartame was assailed in other quarters. The first problem is phenylketonuria (PKU). One out of 20,000 babies is born without the ability to metabolize phenylalanine, one of the two amino acids that make up aspartame (and also found in many natural proteins). Toxic levels of this substance in their blood can result in mental retardation. As a result, the FDA requires all packaged goods that contain aspartame to bear a warning notice for the benefit of people with PKU. Some scientists believe that high aspartame intakes (more than a few artificially sweetened foods a day) could pose some risk of mental retardation in the babies of pregnant women who carry the trait for PKU, but do not themselves have the disease. The FDA disputes this claim.

Beyond PKU, there are other safety questions surrounding the use of aspartame. Several scientists are concerned that aspartame might cause altered brain function and behavior changes in consumers. And many people (though a minuscule fraction of those who have consumed the additive) have reported dizziness, headaches, epileptic-like seizures, and menstrual problems after ingesting aspartame. Lawsuits have been filed to block its use, but the courts have upheld the FDA's approval process.

One of the controversies plaguing aspartame is a rat study that found a somewhat increased risk of brain tumors. A second study did not find such an increase, but that study used a different strain of rat, so it didn't remove the concern. Because aspartame is so widely used, the FDA should have required the manufacturer to conduct a more definitive study years ago.

If you're overweight, it is unlikely that aspartame or other artificial sweeteners will help you slim down. The best way to lose weight—and keep it off—is to exercise regularly and eat lots of low-fat, low-calorie foods, such as vegetables, whole-wheat bread, pasta with tomato (not a creamy) sauce, and fresh fruit. Also, keep plenty of fresh, low-calorie snacks around your house or office and eliminate "junk foods." These measures will ultimately be much more effective than diet drinks or roller-coaster fad diets.

◆ **Safe Food choice:** Avoid aspartame if you are pregnant, suffer from PKU, or think that you experience side effects from using it. If you consume more than a couple of servings a day, consider cutting back. And, to be on the safe side, don't give aspartame to infants.

BHA

BHA and BHT (see below) are two closely related chemicals that are added to oil-containing foods to prevent oxidation and to retard rancidity. Until the early 1980s, BHA (butylated hydroxyanisole) was firmly ensconced on the FDA's list of additives that are "Generally Recognized as Safe" (GRAS). But in 1982, a Japanese researcher found that BHA induced tumors in the forestomachs of rats. While humans don't have forestomachs, any kind of animal tumor is cause for concern. The International Agency for Research on Cancer, part of the World Health Organization, considers BHA to be possibly carcinogenic to humans, and the State of California has listed it as a carcinogen. The FDA is currently reviewing its approval of BHA. Meanwhile, the additive appears in hundreds of processed foods, such as potato chips, presweetened cereals, and bouillon cubes.

◆ **Safe Food choice:** To avoid BHA, simply read the label. If it's in the product, it's listed.

BHT

BHT (butylated hydroxytoluene) has been the subject of numerous tests that have yielded divergent results,

Chemical cuisine

Here are some of the additives that you're most likely to run across on food labels. Most of these are safe.

Key:
   ✗ Everyone should avoid
   △ Certain people should avoid
   ? Needs more testing
   ✄ Cut back on this

✗ acesulfame K
(artificial sweetener)

alginate, propylene glycol alginate
(thickening agents; foam stabilizer)

alpha tocopherol (vitamin E)
(antioxidant, nutrient)

✗ artificial colorings

? artificial flavorings

ascorbic acid (vitamin C)
(antioxidant, nutrient, color stabilizer)

?△ aspartame
(artificial sweetener)

beta carotene
(coloring; nutrient)

✗ butylated hydroxyanisole
(BHA)
(antioxidant)

✗ butylated hydroxytoluene
(BHT)
(antioxidant)

△ caffeine
(stimulant)

calcium (or sodium) propionate
(preservative)

calcium (or sodium) stearoyl lactylate
(dough conditioner, whipping agent)

carrageenan
(thickening and stabilizing agent)

casein, sodium caseinate
(thickening and whitening agent)

citric acid, sodium citrate
(acid, flavoring, preservative)

✄ corn syrup
(sweetener, thickener)

✄ dextrose (glucose, corn sugar)
(sweetener, coloring agent)

EDTA
(preservative)

erythorbic acid
(antioxidant)

ferrous gluconate
(coloring, nutrient)

fumaric acid
(tartness agent)

gelatin
(thickening and gelling agent)

glycerin (glycerol)
(maintains water content)

gums—arabic, guar, etc.
(thickening agents, stabilizers)

? heptyl paraben
(preservative)

✄ high-fructose corn syrup
(sweetener, thickener)

? hydrogenated vegetable oil
(source of oil or fat)

△ hydrolyzed vegetable protein
(HVP)
(flavoring similar to MSG)

✄ invert sugar
(sweetener)

lactic acid
(acidity regulator)

lactose
(sweetener)

lecithin
(emulsifier, antioxidant)

mannitol
(sweetener)

mono- and diglycerides
(emulsifier)

△ monosodium glutamate
(MSG)
(flavoring)

✄ phosphoric acid; phosphates
(acidulant, preservative,
buffer, emulsifier, discoloration inhibitor)

polysorbate 60
(emulsifier)

?✗ propyl gallate
(antioxidant)

? quinine
(flavoring)

✗ saccharin
(artificial sweetener)

✄ salt (sodium chloride)
(flavoring)

sodium benzoate
(preservative)

sodium carboxymethylcellu-
lose (CMC)
(thickening and stabilizing
agent; prevents sugar from
crystallizing)

✗ sodium nitrite, sodium nitrate
(preservative, coloring, flavoring)

sorbic acid, potassium sorbate
(prevents growth of mold)

sorbitan monostearate
(emulsifier)

sorbitol
(sweetener, thickening agent,
maintains moisture)

starch, modified starch
(thickening agent)

✄ sugar (sucrose)
(sweetener)

△ sulfites (sulfur dioxide, sodium
bisulfite, etc.)
(preservative, bleach)

vanillin, ethyl vanillin
(substitutes for vanilla)

including conflicting reports on its cancer-inducing ability. Some studies show reduced incidence of tumors with
addition of BHT; some show increased incidence. BHA
and BHT are both entirely unnecessary. They prolong
the shelf life of foods, but
there are plenty of safer
alternatives.

In some cases,
dark bottles miti-
gate the need for
chemical preser-
vatives. In some
bottled foods, the air
can be replaced by nitro-
gen gas. Vitamins C and E are
effective antioxidants (though a tad more expensive than
BHA and BHT). In foods where BHA or BHT are added
as "insurance," no preservative at all is needed. On grocery-store shelves you will frequently find brands of food
that have no synthetic preservatives right next to competi-
tors that do.

◆ **Safe Food choice:** Read the label. Because of the
possibility that it might increase the risk of cancer, BHT
should be phased out of our food supply. To play it safe,
phase it out of your diet.

CAFFEINE

Caffeine is found naturally in tea, coffee, and cocoa,
and is added to many soft drinks. It is one of the only
drugs—a stimulant—added to foods. It promotes stom-
ach-acid secretion (possibly increasing symptoms of peptic
ulcers), temporarily raises blood pressure, and dilates
some blood vessels while constricting others. Excessive
caffeine intake results in a condition called "caffeinism,"
with symptoms ranging from nervousness and jitteriness
to insomnia. A study at the National Institute of Mental

Health showed that 8- to 13-year-old boys who normally did not consume caffeine experienced restlessness, nervousness, nausea, and insomnia after consuming the caffeine equivalent of either two or seven cans of soft drinks.[4] Because of differences in body weight, the amount of caffeine in a 12-ounce soft drink has about the same impact on a child as the caffeine in a 6-ounce cup of coffee has on an adult.

Caffeine may also interfere with reproduction and affect developing fetuses. Experiments with laboratory animals link caffeine to birth defects such as cleft palates, missing fingers and toes, and skull malformations. Some of these problems result after hefty intakes of 20 or more cups of coffee per day, but one study showed that the equivalent of three cups per day delayed bone growth.[5] In 1980, CSPI sponsored a Caffeine and Birth Defects Clearinghouse in order to find children affected by caffeine. CSPI's report of three children who were born with missing fingers or toes was published in the British medical journal, *The Lancet*. Each of these children's mothers drank eight or more cups of coffee per day. Several human studies have shown that caffeine does not pose a big risk, but they could not rule out small risks. The FDA has advised that "Pregnant women should avoid caffeine-containing foods and drugs, if possible, or consume them only sparingly."

Caffeine may also cause or aggravate fibrocystic breast disease (benign breast lumps) in some women. Breast lumps are sometimes painful and can be dangerous because they could hide malignant lumps. John Minton, M.D., of Ohio State University, published several studies indicating that breast lumps occurred much less frequently after women stopped consuming caffeine. Other studies have found no link.[6]

Caffeine is mildly addictive, which is why many people experience headaches when they stop consuming caffeine. Its addictiveness is probably one reason why soft-drink manufacturers like to add it to their products, though it also contributes to the flavor. (Caffeine isn't just in cola drinks, either—the soft drinks Mountain Dew and Mellow Yellow have somewhat higher caffeine levels than Coca-Cola.)

One good thing can be said about caffeine: It doesn't appear to initiate or promote cancer.

◆ **Safe Food choice:** While small amounts of caffeine don't pose a problem for everyone, avoid it if you are (or are trying to become)[7] pregnant. If you tend to develop benign breast lumps, it's certainly worth avoiding caffeine for a few months to see if they disappear. And try to keep caffeine out of your child's diet.

MONOSODIUM GLUTAMATE (MSG)

Early in this century, a Japanese chemist identified monosodium glutamate (MSG) as the substance in certain seasonings that added to the flavor of protein-containing foods. Soon Japanese firms began producing it commercially, and people around the world were adding MSG to everything from soup to nuts.

Unfortunately, too much MSG can lead to headaches, tightness in the chest, and a burning sensation in the forearms and the back of the neck. These symptoms, called the "Chinese restaurant syndrome," were identified in 1968 and linked to soup served in Chinese restaurants. Soup is a particular problem, because it often contains large doses of MSG and tends to be consumed on an empty stomach—which means the MSG will be readily absorbed into the blood.

The MSG industry has frequently claimed that reactions to MSG are overrated or even nonexistent. However, Robert Kenny, Ph.D., of George Washington University, has conducted industry-sponsored research proving that many people do react to MSG. The higher the dose, the greater the likelihood of reacting. (Kenny also found that many people who thought they were sensitive to MSG were not.)

George Schwartz, M.D., a New Mexico physician, has waged a campaign to rid the food supply of MSG. His organization, "NO MSG," urges that MSG be banished from the food supply, or at least that its presence be disclosed on all processed foods in which it's used. Schwartz and his colleagues have publicly objected to the fact that the USDA has permitted some companies to include MSG and a related additive, HVP (hydrolyzed vegetable protein), under the general term "artificial flavorings."

◆ **Safe Food choice:** If you think you are sensitive to MSG, look at ingredient listings carefully. Also, avoid hydrolyzed vegetable protein, or HVP, which may contain MSG. The organization NO MSG can provide additional information (see page 209).

NITRITE AND NITRATE

Sodium nitrite and sodium nitrate are two closely related chemicals that have been used for centuries to preserve meat. They maintain the meat's red color, contribute to its flavor, and inhibit the growth of potentially dangerous botulism-causing bacteria. While nitrate itself is harmless, it is readily converted—by bacterial action in foods, and in the body—to nitrite. When nitrite combines with compounds called secondary amines, it forms nitrosamines, extremely powerful cancer-causing

Other additives to watch out for

Aside from our "Top 10 additives to subtract from your diet," other additives may pose risks:

➤ **Quinine** is a fairly potent drug used to treat malaria, and it is used in quinine water. It has never been adequately tested, especially for birth defects.

➤ **Propyl gallate** is an antioxidant that is closely related to BHA and BHT. It caused cancer in one animal study, and should be eliminated from the food supply.

➤ **Potassium bromate** (see page 65) could pose a cancer risk if it persists in bread.

chemicals. The chemical reaction occurs most readily at the high temperatures of frying, but may also occur to some degree in the stomach.

Nitrite hit the headlines in 1972 when CSPI published a report subtitled "Don't Bring Home the Bacon." The report informed the public about nitrosamines, especially in bacon. Bacon is a special problem, since it is thinly sliced and fried at a high temperature. Hot dogs, bologna, ham, and other processed meats pose less of a risk, at least in this respect.

Philip Hartman, Ph.D., of Johns Hopkins University, has hypothesized that nitrite has long been a significant cause of stomach cancer in the United States, Japan, and elsewhere. He has correlated dietary levels of nitrite with the rate of this cancer. The Japanese, he notes, consume high levels of nitrite and suffer one of the highest rates of stomach cancer in the world. In the United States, the rate of stomach cancer has been declining for 60 years. Hartman has found that as refrigeration reduced the need for nitrite and nitrate preservatives, and as diets have changed, Americans have been eating less of those preservatives.

In the 1970s, following pressure from CSPI and Ralph Nader's Center for Study of Responsive Law, the USDA banned nitrate from most processed meats. It also lowered the permitted levels of nitrite, and required bacon processors to use ascorbic acid (or its close, safe relative, erythorbic acid) in curing. The ascorbic acid inhibits the formation of nitrosamines. The nitrosamine

Safe doses

Many foods are fortified with vitamins and minerals. But if you take vitamin and mineral supplements, keep in mind that some—such as vitamins A, D, B6, and the minerals zinc and selenium—can be unsafe if taken in megadoses. For example, megadoses of vitamin A may cause birth defects. Check with your doctor before taking vitamin or mineral megadoses. The book *The Right Dose* has information on safe doses of vitamins and minerals (see page 206).

problem is considerably less serious than it was 20 years ago, but bacon is still all too often contaminated. USDA-sponsored research has developed a way to totally eliminate the need for nitrite in bacon, but the USDA has failed to require the meat industry to adopt it. The meat industry says it needs nitrite as a preservative, but it is really more concerned about marketing products with a cosmetically acceptable appearance and familiar taste.

It's worth noting that much of the nitrite that we are exposed to is produced naturally in the body, or comes from nitrate-containing vegetables that have been stored too long. This still doesn't justify intentionally adding nitrite to our food.

◆ **Safe Food choice:** Look for nitrite-free processed meats—some of which are frozen—at some health-food and grocery stores, if you want to buy these products. But regardless of the presence of nitrite or nitrosamines, the high-fat, high-sodium content of most processed meats should be enough to discourage you from choosing them. And don't cook with bacon drippings.

SACCHARIN

This sugar substitute has been used for nearly a century as a noncaloric sweetener. Until the early 1970s it seemed that saccharin's only drawback was its unpleasant, bitter aftertaste. But then several studies linked saccharin with cancer in laboratory animals, which provoked the government to remove it from the list of chemicals that are "Generally Recognized as Safe" (GRAS). After further studies, in 1977, the FDA decided to ban saccharin. But public opposition was enormous. Thousands of consumers wanted to continue buying saccharin-sweetened diet foods, and demanded that Congress override the FDA's decision. The flames of consumer revolt were fanned by industry's advertisements. Congress responded by interceding and exempting saccharin from regular

165

food-safety laws, and by 1991, the exemption had been extended several times. For better or worse, aspartame has replaced saccharin in many foods. Regardless of whether saccharin helps people lose weight—and there's little evidence that it does—food manufacturers love saccharin for several reasons. It's cheaper than sugar—although diet products can be priced the same or even higher than nondiet products, thus increasing profits. Also, having diet versions of their products gives manufacturers twice the shelf space in supermarkets, increasing their exposure.

◆ **Safe Food choice:** Avoid saccharin. Sweetener packets and cans of saccharin-containing diet drinks bear warning labels: "Use of this product may be hazardous to your health. This product contains saccharin, which has been determined to cause cancer in laboratory animals." Why not heed the warning?

SULFITES

Sulfites are a class of chemicals that can keep cut fruits and vegetables looking fresh, even when they're not. Sulfites also prevent discoloration in apricots, raisins, and other dried fruits; control "black spot" in freshly caught shrimp; and prevent discoloration, bacterial growth, and fermentation of wine.

Sulfites, or sulfur dioxide gas, have been used for centuries and were always considered safe. Their one flaw was thought to be their ability to destroy thiamin (vitamin B1), which is one reason sulfites have never been permitted in meat or other sources of thiamin. In 1982 the FDA proposed that sulfites officially be declared "Generally Recognized as Safe." But shortly thereafter, CSPI found six scientific studies published in the previous few years proving that sulfites could provoke sometimes severe allergic reactions.

Sulfite sensitivity was first discovered by Bruce Prenner, M.D., and John Stevens, M.D., allergists at the University of California at San Diego. CSPI quickly asked the FDA to ban all unnecessary uses of sulfites.

CSPI's request to ban sulfites generated tremendous publicity and prompted several people to report the possibility of sulfite-related deaths. Ultimately, CSPI and the FDA identified at least a dozen fatalities linked to this food additive. A typical reaction is difficulty breathing within minutes of consuming sulfites. Most of the reactions and all of the deaths occurred among asthmatics, although only 5 to 10 percent of asthmatics are sulfite-sensitive. Researchers theorize that sulfite-sensitive individuals lack the ability to convert sulfite to harmless sulfate.

In 1985, Congress finally forced the FDA to ban sulfites from most fresh fruits and vegetables. The FDA also ordered makers of numerous processed foods that contained sulfites to list the additive on the label, as the law had always required.

◆ **Safe Food choice:** Especially if you have asthma, be sure to consider whether your attacks might be related to sulfites and sulfite-containing foods. The ban on sulfites doesn't cover fresh-cut potatoes, dried fruits, and wine. If you are sulfite-sensitive, look for potato products, dried fruits, and wines produced without sulfites. People who are not sensitive to sulfites, whether or not they have asthma, need not be concerned.

THE DELANEY DEBATE

One of the longest-standing controversies related to food additives revolves around a 1958 law that regulates their use. This law, the Delaney amendment (named after its chief sponsor, Congressman James J. Delaney), bans the use of any food additive that has been found to cause cancer in animals or humans. Though the law has rarely been enforced, food and chemical manufacturers have lobbied for years to have it revoked. Companies fear that minuscule amounts of a useful additive could be banned, even if the additive caused few or no cancers in the general population. That is certainly a theoretical possibility: some flavorings, for instance, are used rarely and in very small amounts, and might be estimated to cause, perhaps, one cancer in 10 billion people. In theory, at least, the Delaney amendment could be called upon to ban such additives.

In practice, the FDA has permitted non-cancer-causing additives to be used, even if they contained small amounts of cancer-causing contaminants. FDA has also allowed packaging materials that increase slightly the risk of cancer. And it has bent over backwards to permit the use of regular additives for which some significant evidence of carcinogenicity exists.

The FDA and industry would like to loosen the law to legalize additives that are estimated to cause fewer than one cancer over the lifetimes of one million people. That amounts to about four cancer deaths a year in the United States. We believe, however, that it just doesn't make sense to knowingly add chemicals to our food supply that promote cancer even slightly—particularly when the chemicals serve a largely cosmetic purpose, such as coloring, flavoring, or thickening a food.

Quite possibly, a chemical that causes only rare cancers in animals might pose a greater threat to some or all humans. After all, thalidomide appeared to be relatively safe based on animal studies. What's more, laboratory tests customarily use well-nourished animals. But humans who are poorly nourished, addicted to drugs or alcohol, chain-smoke, suffer from asthma or diabetes, take various medications, or are exposed to various pollutants may be much more susceptible to a particular chemical than the animals tested. The point to remember: for virtually all of the additives now suspected of causing cancer, reasonable substitutes are available.

WHAT YOU CAN DO ABOUT ADDITIVES

◆ Complain to makers of additive-laden food. Pressure from parents who thought their children were reacting to additives spurred a number of companies to remove artificial colorings and other questionable additives from their products. Thank companies whose products do not contain additives you're concerned about.

◆ Urge your Senators and your Representative to demand tougher testing of additives and more vigorous enforcement of the food-additive laws: Additives should be licensed for, say, 20 years, rather than being approved permanently. The license could be renewed only if safety tests of the additive met current standards. Additives should be tested both alone and in combination with a mixture of chemicals that people often consume—such as caffeine, birth-control pills, aspirin, anti-hypertension medications, etc. Additives should also be tested on animals with nutrient deficiencies and other medical conditions relevant to human beings. Once additives are permitted in the general food supply, their ability to cause behavioral and allergic reactions in humans should be monitored systematically.

◆ Urge legislators to retain the Delaney amendment.

ADDITIVES OF THE FUTURE

With more consumers than ever before concerned about fatty foods and obesity, food and chemical manufacturers are working overtime to develop new additives to substitute for fat and sugar.

Fat substitutes have permitted dramatic declines in the fat and calorie content of processed foods ranging from mayonnaise to ice cream to cake. Simplesse, an additive developed by the NutraSweet Company, is made largely from milk or egg protein. It is being used in fat-free frozen desserts that resemble ice cream, but it cannot be used to fry foods, because it would coagulate. Other companies, such as Kraft General Foods, are using various vegetable gums to replace fat. And McDonald's is using water and carrageenan, a safe substance made from seaweed, to replace much of the fat in McLean Deluxe hamburger meat. All of these fat substitutes are safe.

Olestra, a sucrose polyester made by Procter & Gamble, represents another kind of fat substitute. It is a greasy, synthetic substance that is not absorbed by the body. Its great advantage over the naturally derived additives is that it can be heated and thus used in frying. Its disadvantage, though, is that it has caused worrisome liver changes and tumors in rats. CSPI has urged the FDA not to approve olestra until all safety questions have been resolved.

Sugar substitutes have a dismal history. Dulcin was banned in 1950 and cyclamate in 1970 as cancer threats. Saccharin appears to increase slightly the risk of cancer. Aspartame may cause occasional mental and physical problems. Acesulfame K (Sunette) was approved in 1988 over CSPI's objections that it caused cancer in rats.

Despite the problematic past of artificial sweeteners, the lucrative diet-food market continues to tempt chemists to create new and, hopefully, safer sugar substitutes. The FDA is now evaluating the safety of two more artificial sweeteners, sucralose and alitame. Sucralose doesn't seem to cause cancer, but it may cause other problems that would limit the number of foods in which it could be used. Alitame hasn't yet been linked to any problem.

What other additives the future will bring is anyone's guess. Some companies are developing salt substitutes. And it is clear that more and more processed foods will be relying on additives to cut back on calories, fat, and sugar. Let's just be sure that the new ingredients are safe, and that the foods and diets they lead to are truly healthful.

CHAPTER 8

THE SAFE FOOD KITCHEN

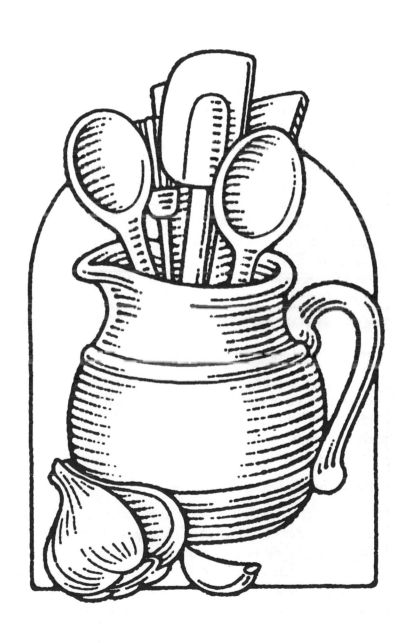

THE SAFE FOOD KITCHEN

The fragrance of dill and sweet basil rising from a pot of soup on the stove, fresh bread warming in the oven, a bowl of lemons on the counter—nothing speaks of warmth and security more than the kitchen. This room is, for most families, the heart of the household. In this chapter, we'll show you how to make it safer.

Whether you've been cooking all your life, or just setting up your first kitchen, if you're cooking for yourself or a whole brood, you'll learn things here you never learned in home economics class—how to buy safe food in a risky marketplace and how to store it properly, what equipment and supplies you need for safe food preparation, and how to use your appliances, including the microwave, to help keep you and your family healthy. *Bon appétit!*

SHOPPING FOR THE SAFE FOOD KITCHEN

HOW TO READ A FOOD LABEL

You're standing in the middle of a grocery-store aisle, carefully studying a food label—and still you haven't a clue about whether the ingredients listed there are nutritious—not to mention safe. Take heart—most food labels are going to get better.

New labeling law to the rescue

Under a new federal law, the Nutrition Labeling and Education Act of 1990, the FDA is going to be overhauling food labeling requirements to give us more accurate, useful information on the nutrition value of our food. For one thing, detailed nutrition labeling will be required on most packaged foods (right now it's required only if a

product makes nutritional claims or if it has been fortified). Labels will have to list several important things,
including the total calories and calories from fat in a typical serving; the amounts of total fat and saturated fat,
cholesterol, sodium, sugars, dietary fiber, carbohydrates,
important vitamins and minerals, and other components;
and the percentage of fruit or vegetable juice contained in
beverages.

The FDA will also establish strict guidelines for
health and nutrition claims on packages. Terms such as
"low-fat" and "light" will be standardized, and nutrition
claims will be better regulated so as not to be misleading.
For example, a product will no longer be allowed to be
labeled "no cholesterol" if it's high in saturated fat.

Unfortunately, all of this applies only to food regulated by the FDA, not the USDA. So it doesn't include
meat and poultry, meat products—such as hot dogs, luncheon meats, sausage, and canned meats—or even frozen
pizzas or frozen dinners that contain meat or poultry.
These prepared foods comprise 20 percent of the food
supply, and are some of the fattiest, saltiest foods we eat.
The new labeling requirements also won't apply to some
$75 billion a year worth of fast foods. Meat and poultry
labeling will eventually be changed too, but the USDA's
new regulations may be very different from the FDA's.

Until then, "Help!"

The FDA's new regulations are required by 1992; the
"all new, improved" labels won't appear on products until
1993. Meanwhile, you'll still have to contend with the
same old confusing labels. Here's some help for the next
time you find yourself squinting at a food label:

◆ First, keep in mind that all **ingredients** are listed
in descending order according to weight. So if water and
sugar are listed first in a product, the product contains
mostly water and sugar.

◆ Pay careful attention to the **serving size.** This can vary from product to product (even within the same type of food), and it might not accurately represent the serving size you use.

◆ The term **no cholesterol** may not mean much on oils, margarines, breads, or pastries, since dietary cholesterol is found only in foods of animal origin, not in food from plants. What's more telling is whether a product is high in saturated fat, which raises blood cholesterol levels. Until the FDA changes its regulations, even products with highly saturated palm oil and coconut oil can claim to be "cholesterol-free."

◆ Check the **fat** level. An adult whose daily diet provides 2,200 calories should consume no more than about 50 grams of fat. Just one serving of Stouffer's chicken enchiladas would provide more than half of that much fat. To find out the percentage of fat calories in a product, use the formula on page 26. Remember, your overall diet goal should be to reduce your intake of calories from fat to about 20 percent or less, and to reduce saturated fat to about 7 percent or less. Fat should certainly account for no more than 30 percent, and saturated fat less than 10 percent of all the calories you consume, whether you are at your ideal weight or not.

◆ **Food additives** must be listed on labels, but sometimes it's hard to recognize them. For instance, MSG, to which some people are sensitive, must be listed, but not when it is contained in another ingredient, such as hydrolyzed vegetable protein. Until the new labeling law goes into effect, food dyes don't have to be named individually. The only exception is Yellow No. 5, which must be listed because it can cause allergic reactions in some people. (For more on additives, see Chapter 7.)

◆ The term **light** or **lite** used on processed meat means that the product has at least 25 percent less fat than usual; on other foods, until the new FDA regulations go into effect, it can refer to almost anything—including light taste, color, or texture, or reduced calories or alcohol content. Check the nutrition label carefully for calorie, fat, and sodium content, and compare it to similar products.

◆ Products labeled **low-calorie** can have no more than 40 calories per serving and no more than 0.4 calories per gram of food. A **reduced-calorie** product must have at least one-third fewer calories than the food it is being compared to.

◆ Right now, the term **natural** doesn't mean much. When used on poultry and meat products, it means "minimally processed and free of artificial ingredients" (such as colorings and nitrite in processed meat). It does not mean, however, that the livestock or poultry it came from were raised without antibiotics or growth hormones. The FDA does not have a definition of "natural" for packaged foods.

◆ No national standards exist for what can be labeled **organic,** though about half the states have their own standards, which sometimes conflict. Under new federal legislation, that will be changing. Until the new standards go into effect in late 1993, check that the organic food you buy has been certified by a certifying organization.

◆ **Sodium free** means less than 5 milligrams (mg) of sodium per serving. **Very low sodium** means the product contains 35 mg or less; **low sodium** means 140 mg or less, and **reduced sodium** simply means the usual level of sodium has been reduced by at least 75 percent—and the product usually is quite salty to begin with (as in most . canned soups). No salt added means a food has no sodium chloride (table salt). However, the food may be high in sodium from sodium benzoate, sodium phosphate, or many other sodium-containing additives. Check the label for sodium content. An adult should aim for about 2,000 mg (or less) of sodium. One 10-ounce serving of Campbell's Chicken Noodle Soup would fill more than half of your sodium allotment.

UNLEADED, PLEASE

Lead is extremely dangerous—especially for children and fetuses—even at very low levels of exposure. So make every effort to eliminate lead from your family's diet. Drinking water is one source of dietary lead (see Chapter 6); so are some pottery and ceramic containers, lead-soldered food cans, and leaded crystal.

Lead in ceramics and pottery. Most ceramic dinnerware is coated with a glaze containing lead. If the glaze is properly formulated, applied, and fired, no lead should leach out of the final product. But if any steps are performed improperly, lead may leach into food. The problem is most likely to occur with imports and handmade pottery or ceramic ware. There's no way to tell if a piece will leach lead just by looking at it, but you can avoid problems in several ways.

Safe Food choices

◆ Put away or just display your grandmother's antique serving dish, collectible painted dinnerware, and other old ceramic objects; don't use them for food or beverages. The FDA only started regulating lead in dishware in 1971, so ceramic cups, bowls, and dishes made before that time may not be safe. One exception is china, including the imported kind, since china must be fired at high temperatures, which would make it safe.

◆ Don't cook, prepare, or serve food in imported lead or ceramic pottery or cookware—or in handcrafted pottery. These objects may be wonderful to look at, but they may not be safe for food. If you have any doubts about an imported or handmade pot or bowl, feast your eyes and show it off, but don't cook your supper in it.

◆ Consider testing your antique or imported ceramic ware with a home-test kit. Two you can use, according to *Consumer Reports*,[1] are Leadcheck Swabs (HybriVet Systems, Inc., P. O. Box 1210, Framingham, MA 01701) and Frandon Lead Alert Kit (Frandon Enterprises, 511 N. 48th St., Seattle, WA 98103). They cost $25 to $30, and a positive finding can alert you to high lead levels in ceramics, as well as paint or even lead-soldered cans. The main drawback is that a negative finding does not necessarily mean the the product is safe, because the test is not extremely sensitive.

Lead in cans. Cans containing lead are becoming rare. Less than 3 percent of domestic food cans contain lead solder, according to a 1990 survey by the National Food Processors Association. But that still amounts to more than 400 million cans. An unknown, but probably much greater, percentage of imported cans contain lead solder. (According to the food processors' survey, companies reported using lead-soldered cans for pet food, fish, vegetable oil, and peanut butter. They also said that they import a variety of food in lead-soldered cans, including mushrooms, fruits, fish, tomatoes, artichokes, pimentos, water chestnuts, and plum pudding.)

Earth-friendly shopping tips

Rules of thumb for choosing the best packaging:

◆ Buy the least amount of packaging for the most product, and buy packaging that is recyclable in your area.

◆ Buy eggs in molded pulp cartons, which are usually made of recycled material, instead of plastic foam containers.

◆ Avoid aseptic juice boxes; they're virtually unrecyclable because of the different layers of paper, plastic, and metal.

◆ As far as possible, avoid buying toxic household cleaners and pesticides. Never store these near food, or within reach of children.

Safe Food choices

◆ Your best bet is to choose canned food only in seamless cans or cans with welded seams (which never use lead), not in cans with soldered seams. Be on the lookout especially if you're buying fish, vegetable oil, or any imported canned food. (The solder may not in fact be lead, but there's no easy way to tell.) Seamless cans are easy to spot; it's a little more challenging to tell the difference between welded and soldered cans. Carefully examine cans with seams. Welded seams are very neat, and the metal around them is shiny. Run your finger down the seam of the can; if you feel unevenness through the label, the seam is soldered, possibly with lead.

◆ Don't store acidic foods, such as tomatoes or citrus juices, in cans after they have been opened. If there is any lead in the solder, the acid and oxygen help it to dissolve and leach into food. Obviously, it would be a lot easier and safer if lead solder were simply banned.

MORE SHOPPING TIPS

◆ Plan ahead when you shop to be sure you have enough refrigerator and freezer space for the fish, meat, and poultry you're buying.

◆ Buy food in undamaged containers and packages—don't buy anything in bulging cans, or jars with cracks or bulging lids (these may be signs of botulism contamination). Paper and plastic packages shouldn't have tears, leaks, or stains.

◆ Shop for meat and poultry last, keep them from touching or dripping juices on other foods, and get them home and into your refrigerator as quickly as possible—within no more than two hours.

◆ Buy frozen products only if they're frozen solid, and buy eggs and products labeled "keep refrigerated" only if they are stored in a refrigerator case at the grocery store.

◆ Observe expiration dates—"fresh-until," "sell-by," or "use-by" dates—on all products.

◆ Buy unbleached coffee filters instead of bleached filters, which may contain tiny amounts of dioxins. (Although the amount of dioxins you're drinking in your coffee isn't anything to lose sleep over, the bleaching process pollutes the environment with dioxins.)

◆ Unless you eat dioxin-contaminated fish (see page 124), your biggest risk from dioxins in food may come from eating fatty foods off paper plates or from cooking fatty frozen foods in paper trays. So your best bet is to choose low-fat foods and avoid using paper plates—the paper waste isn't good for the environment, either. Questions have also been raised about dioxins leaching from milk cartons into milk. Fortunately, that problem is being resolved. The levels of any dioxins in milk were tiny to begin with, and the FDA has asked for manufacturing changes to reduce the levels even further.

STORING FOOD IN THE
SAFE FOOD KITCHEN

Nothing's more annoying than looking forward to that piece of toast or juicy tomato or homemade preserves and finding it tainted by mold. Refrigeration has greatly reduced that sort of food spoilage, but it still happens to the best of us whose appetites can't quite devour the contents of our refrigerators on schedule. Here are some tips to prevent food spoilage and to help you decide whether or not it's safe to eat spoiled food.

IN YOUR REFRIGERATOR OR FREEZER

◆ Keep your refrigerator and freezer cold enough to store food safely—no warmer than 40 degrees F for your refrigerator, no warmer than 0 degrees for your freezer. Don't keep them colder than necessary either, since that wastes enormous amounts of energy. Most refrigerators and freezers simply have "colder" and "warmer" settings, so you can't tell how cold they are. Buy a thermometer (any thermometer with the right temperature ranges will do), and run tests on the refrigerator and freezer, then adjust the settings until you achieve the proper temperatures.

◆ If your freezer is jam-packed and frozen over, it isn't working as well as it could. Defrost it, and discard old, ice-covered goods. Date the packages you save and place them in front of the freezer for early use.

◆ Put leftovers in your refrigerator as soon as possible. Leaving hot foods out to cool at room temperature just invites bacteria to multiply. Store leftovers to be chilled in the smallest containers possible, and transfer food from hot cooking pots into cool storage containers. To refrigerate a large pot of very hot food—such as soup or stew—submerge the pot in a sinkful of ice water, stir

How healthy are health-food stores?

Health-food and natural-food stores generally offer many nutritious foods that are unavailable at much larger supermarkets. However, just because something is sold at a health-food store doesn't guarantee that it's healthy.

Some products to avoid include "health" bars loaded with fat; raw-sugar products, such as Sucanat, which is advertised as being loaded with vitamins and minerals but is little better than table sugar or brown sugar; raw milk and raw cheese, which can cause food poisoning; and comfrey and coltsfoot teas that might promote cancer.

Shop at health-food stores the way you should shop at other stores: carefully!

the food for several minutes, and when it stops steaming, refrigerate it in small containers.

◆ Keep in mind that fresh poultry will only keep one to two days in your refrigerator, and fresh meat three to five days. Fish should be used within one day. Most leftovers will keep about three to four days. Vacuum-packed meats such as luncheon meats can last two weeks unopened, and five to seven days opened.

◆ In warm weather consider keeping whole-grain flour, crackers, and bread in the refrigerator or freezer.

◆ If you lose electrical power and your refrigerator goes off, keep the door closed and within a few hours either cook the food or move it into someone else's refrigerator. Since temperature and climate conditions vary, call the USDA Meat and Poultry Hotline at 1-800-535-4555 for specific help about what foods can be kept, and what to throw out.

IN YOUR CUPBOARD OR PANTRY

◆ Keep canned goods in a cool, dry place—not above your stove, under the sink, or in a garage or basement. Keep food in safe places, away from pets, household cleaners and other chemicals, and not near pipes or seeping moisture. (Under the sink, leaky pipes can drip on food, causing mold and spoilage. Pipes are also a typical entrance for roaches and mice.)

◆ Low-acid commercially canned foods, including most vegetables except tomatoes, can last two years or longer if they're stored in a cool, dry place, and if the cans are in good condition—that is, if they have no dents, holes, rust, bulges, or leaks. Under good conditions, high-acid canned goods (including tomato products, and most fruit and fruit juices) can last 18 months.

◆ When you bring home new canned goods from the store, rotate the old ones to the front to use first, or date cans and use the older ones first.

WHAT TO DO ABOUT MOLDS

◆ Don't smell moldy food—some molds can cause respiratory problems. Instead, if the food is very moldy, wrap it up and discard it. Clean up the refrigerator where it was sitting, and look at other foods nearby to be sure the mold didn't spread.

◆ You can cut away small moldy spots on hard cheese, salami, and firm fruits and vegetables (such as cabbage, bell peppers, and carrots). Keep your knife out of the mold and cut out about an inch-wide square around and below the mold (invisible spores spread out from the visibly moldy part). Put the food in a clean storage container, cover it with fresh wrap, or use it immediately.

◆ You can safely scoop out tiny spots of mold from jelly or jam. Then, with a clean spoon, scoop out a larger area around the spot. If the jam tastes fermented, throw it out.

◆ Throw out any of the following foods if they are even slightly moldy: individual cheese slices, soft cheese, cottage cheese, cream, sour cream, yogurt, bread, cake, buns, pastry, corn on the cob, nuts, flour, whole grains, rice, dried peas and beans, and peanut butter.

MORE STORAGE TIPS

◆ Your very best choice for storing food: reusable glass or sturdy, reusable plastic containers with tight

---

Cool it

You can save energy (which helps protect the environment and your budget) if you clean the condenser coils on the back or bottom of your refrigerator at least once a year. Also, keep the door gasket clean to make sure the seal isn't being broken.

lids. For storing food, don't reuse plastic food bags that have come into contact with raw meat or poultry; bacteria can accumulate and contaminate your food. Printed plastic bags (such as the ones that bread comes in) may have very high lead levels in the ink used for printing.[2] Although the lead doesn't leach through the plastic into the bread, don't turn the bag inside out and use it for storing any food, since the ink could leach or chip off.

◆ Avoid using plastic wraps in contact with fatty foods, particularly hot fatty foods (such as in the microwave oven—see page 184).

◆ Don't store highly acidic or salty foods, such as tomato sauce, rhubarb, or sauerkraut, in aluminum, since aluminum may leach into the food. Also, don't store acidic foods, such as fruit juices, in imported ceramic containers, since they may leach lead into the food.

PREPARING FOOD IN THE SAFE FOOD KITCHEN

COOKING IN YOUR MICROWAVE

Microwave ovens are now standard kitchen equipment in nearly three-quarters of American homes. In 1987 consumers spent about $1 billion on "microwavable" foods, and by 1992 we are expected to spend some $3 billion annually on packaged food for microwave ovens. Aside from the serious environmental consequences of all the extra packaging-to-be-garbage, are these microwavable foods really safe?

Unless your microwave is very damaged or was made before 1971, you needn't be concerned about microwaves leaking from ovens. No microwave oven is allowed to leak more than 5 milliwatts per square centimeter 2 inches away from the oven—a level that is probably not hazardous. Microwaves made after 1971 have automatic shut-off devices to prevent them from operating when the door is open. The jury is still out on whether exposure to electromagnetic fields from electric appliances, including microwaves, is linked to cancer. But as long as you're not close to an operating microwave oven for long periods, you're safe.

Some packaging used in the microwave is a concern, however—"heat-susceptor" packaging, for one. This type of packaging is used for microwave popcorn and foods such as pizza, waffles, and French fries that need to be browned or "crisped"—something the microwave can't do on its own. A heat-susceptor package has a plastic-coated metal strip or disk which absorbs the microwave energy in the oven and can get as hot as 500 degrees F—turning the package into a veritable frying pan. According to the FDA, the high temperatures cause the package to break down, releasing chemicals from adhesives, polymers, paper, and paperboard into the food. The FDA never considered those temperatures when it initially approved the materials in heat-susceptor packages. According to the FDA, "the revolutionary technologies producing these niceties were applied before the agency's regulations were ready for them."[3]

Testing so far has found low levels of chemicals leaching from some packages into food (though none of some particularly hazardous chemicals the FDA tested for). But the FDA hasn't even identified, much less studied, the health effects of most of the chemicals that migrate from these packages into food.

Plastic "cling" wraps pose another problem. A 1987 British study found that a plasticizer commonly used in some plastic wraps migrates into fatty foods during microwaving and even at temperatures found in the refrigerator when the wrap is in direct contact with the fatty food.[4]

Surprisingly, even when packaging products are labeled "microwavable," or "microwave safe," that doesn't necessarily mean that they are safe for use in the microwave. These are industry claims—the FDA doesn't guarantee them. "Housewares" don't have to meet the same FDA standards as food-product packaging, and there are no standard industry-wide tests to ensure that they won't leach contaminants into your food.

What you can do

◆ Heat-susceptor packages may not have killed anyone, but until these products are properly approved and shown to be safe, your best bet is to avoid them—unless you don't mind a little plastic and glue with your microwaved pizza. Either don't buy these foods, or put them into other containers (preferably oven-proof glass) before you cook them.

◆ Make sure that no foods touch plastic wrap during microwaving. Or just stick to oven-proof glass containers and glass covers. Never use flimsy plastic containers like yogurt cups or margarine tubs in your microwave oven.

More microwaving tips

◆ Use your microwave only if the door closes easily and tightly; don't use it if an object is caught in the door, or if the door is otherwise damaged. If there are any signs of rusting on the oven, have it repaired.

◆ If your children operate your microwave oven, make sure they know how to operate it properly. Teach your kids the importance of cooking foods long enough and handling them carefully. Youngsters have been burned by microwaved jelly doughnuts, since the jelly inside can

---

Bag it

Use cloth or string bags when you go shopping, and you won't have so many plastic bags around the house to begin with! Do reuse plastic bags for taking garbage out—that way you don't have to buy garbage bags. Or return the bags to the supermarket if it has a recycling program.

Good gadgets for the Safe Food kitchen

◆ Thermometers: a meat thermometer for making sure meat and poultry are cooked thoroughly; a microwave-safe thermometer, if you have a microwave oven; and a thermometer for testing your refrigerator and freezer temperatures.

◆ A plastic, marble, or other nonporous cutting board that can be washed thoroughly with hot, soapy water after handling raw meat, poultry, and fish.

◆ A vegetable brush for scrubbing produce.

◆ Cloth or string shopping bags.

◆ Cloth dish rags.

◆ A fat-skimming cup for removing fat from soups and broths.

◆ Reusable, sturdy plastic or glass containers for storage.

◆ A reusable (cotton or gold) coffee filter, or unbleached paper filters.

◆ A set of sharp knives—and a knife sharpener—for trimming meat and fish, and for peeling fruits and vegetables.

◆ An oven-proof glass casserole dish with a cover to use in the microwave.

◆ A heavy-duty, hand can opener that can be washed in hot, soapy water.

be burning hot although the outside dough feels cool. Also, teach them to be careful to avoid burns from steam venting from bags of microwaved popcorn.

◆ To avoid accidents, puncture foods such as potatoes, tomatoes, sausages, etc., before cooking them, and don't use the microwave for deep frying.

◆ To protect infants against burns, never warm baby bottles in the microwave.

◆ Don't be impatient! The most common microwaving mistake is not cooking foods long enough to kill all the bacteria. It is extremely important to cook prepared foods according to instructions, to reheat leftovers thoroughly, and to follow any instructions calling for food to stand after you take it from the oven—this additional time is necessary for the food to finish cooking.

◆ Use special care when microwaving meat, poultry, or fish to ensure that they are cooked thoroughly. De-bone large pieces of meat. Turn meat, poultry, or fish several times during cooking and use a temperature probe or meat thermometer in a few places to check the internal temperature for doneness. Cook both beef and pork to an internal temperature of at least 160 degrees F, so that they are slightly pink inside. Poultry should be cooked to 180 degrees F, and fish to 140 degrees F.

Cover your cooking dish with an oven-proof glass top; the steam that accumulates will heat the surface of the food, helping it to cook more evenly.

The oven of choice

Some prepared foods come with disposable trays that can be used in either a conventional or microwave oven. But these trays may not be particularly safe in conventional ovens. FDA tests found that 10 times more of the contaminant PET migrated into food from these trays when the food was heated in a conventional oven than when heated in a microwave. Before cooking food in your conventional oven, transfer it to a baking pan.

◆ Don't cook whole, stuffed poultry in a microwave oven—the warm, moist conditions in the stuffing combined with uneven cooking create perfect conditions for bacterial growth.

◆ When you defrost food in a microwave, finish cooking it immediately. Also be sure to remove food from store wrap or foam trays before thawing it in a microwave oven.

◆ Don't use your microwave oven for home canning—it cooks too unevenly for that purpose.

◆ Do use your microwave oven to cook vegetables. Microwaving often retains more vitamins and minerals than cooking by conventional methods does, because microwave cooking times are shorter and less water is used.

◆ Do use your microwave to pre-cook meats to minimize heterocyclic amines.

◆ Don't bother investing in a microwave radiation detector. If it costs less than a new microwave oven, it's probably not reliable.

THOSE POTS AND PANS

Ever wonder whether it's safe to use your old scratched-up Teflon pan? And how about the controversy over aluminum pots and Alzheimer's disease? Here's what's safe and what's not in cookware:

◆ **Stainless steel.** Stainless steel appears to be perfectly safe for most people. For a small fraction of people who are allergic to nickel, eating food with a high nickel content—including acidic foods such as stewed tomatoes or rhubarb that has been cooked in stainless-steel cookware—may aggravate the symptoms of dermatitis.[5]

◆ **Cast iron.** This is an excellent choice. It's safe, and can even be a source of needed iron in the diet.

◆ **Copper.** Don't use it if it's unlined. It is okay if it is lined (most good-quality copperware is lined with tin or stainless steel). But if the lining wears out, you'll have to pay to have the pan relined, since acidic foods can cause copper to be released from the cookware into the food. Although our bodies need a little copper, too much can cause nausea, vomiting, and diarrhea.

◆ **Aluminum.** Maybe in 20 years scientists will prove that aluminum causes Alzheimer's disease, and everyone will throw out their aluminum pots and pans. Right now, the evidence linking aluminum to Alzheimer's disease is not strong. Some (not all) Alzheimer's patients have elevated levels of aluminum in their brains, but it isn't clear if that's a cause or an effect of the disease. It does appear that the incidence of Alzheimer's disease is increasing, though, so it is important that more research be done.

◆ **Teflon.** Teflon is an inert material. Although you should avoid scratching the pan with metal utensils, so that you don't eat Teflon particles in your food and don't impair the pan's "nonstick" property, the particles wouldn't be absorbed by your body anyway. Just don't use Teflon cookware for broiling, or leave it unattended at high heat, because it may give off fumes. One advantage to Teflon: you can use less oil.

◆ **Ceramic.** The FDA recommends avoiding ceramic cookware from Mexico, China, India, and Hong Kong, because of the possibility that it may leach dangerous amounts of lead into food.

MORE FOOD-PREPARATION TIPS

◆ Use a different spoon for stirring raw and cooked foods, and don't taste meat, poultry, eggs, fish, or shellfish when they are raw or during cooking—the bacteria in and on the food may still be alive. This includes raw cake and cookie batter containing uncooked eggs.

◆ Marinate foods in the refrigerator, not at room temperature.

◆ Wash dirt and dust from can lids before opening the can—and wash the can opener regularly.

◆ To reheat broths, gravies, soups, and stews, boil them for several minutes to kill any bacteria that may be present.

◆ If you do any home canning, follow instructions scrupulously. Send for the brochure "Home Canning of Fruits and Vegetables," Superintendent of Documents, U.S. Government Printing Office, Washington, D.C. 20402.

◆ For serving food, use warming plates and chafing dishes that maintain the internal temperature at 140 degrees or higher, to prevent bacteria from multiplying.

◆ Never taste suspicious-looking or bad-smelling food.

Earth-friendly kitchen cleaning tips

◆ Cut down on paper towel use. Paper towels use up resources, create waste, and manufacturing bleached paper towels creates dioxins. Having said all this, paper towels may be the best thing for cleaning up after handling raw meat, poultry, fish, and eggs, because they can be thrown away. A good compromise: use paper towels only for these cleanups, and use cloths or dishrags all other times.

◆ Washing the dishes with the water running the whole time can use up more than 30 gallons of water. Rinse your dishes all at once instead. Also, use a low-flow filter on your faucet to cut water waste (but not if you have a portable dishwasher that hooks up to the faucet). An automatic dishwasher uses electricity, but saves water.

◆ And, of course, don't forget to wash your hands with hot, soapy water before and after preparing food.

CLEANING UP THE SAFE FOOD KITCHEN

◆ When it comes to cleaning your safe food kitchen, the word is *often*—particularly after handling raw meat, poultry, fish, and eggs. Use clean washcloths or dish rags—not sponges, since they may harbor bacteria—and launder these often.

◆ Pests such as roaches are a problem in the safe food kitchen, since they can spread germs. But pesticides are also a problem, since they are toxic by design. The Bio-Integral Resource Center publishes excellent materials on the least toxic pest controls (see page 211). For starters, try using boric acid.

◆ Mold can grow at refrigerator temperatures. To help control mold, keep the inside of your refrigerator clean—use one tablespoon of baking soda dissolved in a quart of water, rinse, and dry. Scrub mold off rubber gaskets with three tablespoons of bleach in a quart of water.

CHAPTER 9

THE SAFE FOOD AGENDA

THE SAFE FOOD AGENDA

The consumer's dilemma: How in the world can you even know about—much less protect yourself from—all the pesticides that might be in produce, the additives in processed foods, the toxic industrial chemicals contaminating fish, the drugs lurking in that healthful skim milk, and the salmonella on that chicken?

To some extent, you can protect yourself by being a smart consumer: by buying certified organically grown food, growing your own vegetables, reading labels carefully, and handling and storing foods properly. That all makes sense. But, frankly, you'll never be able to keep up-to-date on every big and little new problem, be it a new type of packaging, a contaminant that makes its way into food, or new research on an old additive.

Ultimately, you've got to rely on the EPA, FDA, and USDA to protect yourself and your loved ones from BHT, EDB, PBB, DDT, and all of the other acronyms and polysyllabic intruders in our food. What to do about big risks, such as smoking or crossing the street without looking both ways, is obvious. To manage smaller risks, our society has established regulatory agencies. The staffs of these agencies are charged with dealing with problems that typical consumers simply don't have enough time or expertise to deal with. Sometimes these agencies don't act quickly or vigorously enough. Sometimes they don't have the legal authority or the budget to cope with certain problems. But they're all we've got, unless Congress steps in and provides more authority and greater funding.

America may have some of the world's safest food, but with thousands of people dying annually from foodborne illnesses, and an unknown number of others being harmed by food additives, pesticides, and small amounts of other toxic chemicals, we should insist on an even safer food supply.

In this chapter, we highlight some of the most pressing food-safety problems that government action could solve. Most of the actions are best done at the national level, but some can be accomplished by local governments or voluntarily by industry. For instance, local governments could insist on better standards of cleanliness in public eating places, nutrition and additive information at restaurants, and signs in grocery stores disclosing the presence of waxes and pesticides on produce. They could provide incentives for establishing community gardens and could reduce the use of pesticides in parks. State governments could levy taxes on pesticides, conduct research on reducing pesticide use, support organic farmers, and help establish farmers' markets in low-income neighborhoods.

But not much will happen without your participation. The chemical and food manufacturers have thousands of employees and full-time lobbyists defending their interests. They contribute to politicians, advertise on television, and "rent" professors. You can bet that they are part of the political process. Lopsided though the battles sometimes seem, you can help tip the balance back in the consumer's favor.

We urge you to get involved in the political process. You and your organizations can also have a direct impact on food suppliers by urging restaurant managers and food processors to use pesticide-free foods and to get rid of questionable additives. You can ask grocers to stock organic foods, to label produce that has been waxed, to provide safer, better-labeled supermarket-brand products, and to stop carrying some of the worst junk foods. You can do all this through meetings, letters, and even boycotts. You can write letters to legislators, write articles for or letters to your local newspapers, volunteer with local activist groups, and join national consumer and environmental groups.

Join the ranks of activists who've made a difference: Carolyn Knight, who helped win a partial ban on sulfite additives; Rosalie Ziomek, who persuaded Chicago-area supermarkets to disclose the use of waxes; and Iowa State Representative David Osterberg, who introduced a law that, among other things, taxes pesticides and fertilizers. It's a wonderful feeling when you see that sometimes you—one lone individual—can have a real impact on the safety of food in your small community, your state, or even the nation.

CLEAN UP CONTAMINATED MEAT AND POULTRY

Our meat supply is endangered by an obsolete inspection system that is overseen by USDA, which sometimes seems more concerned with promoting meat than protecting consumers.

The system is characterized by ridiculously little time to inspect meat and poultry, a focus on appearance rather than health risks from bacteria and drugs, and limited inspection authority.

◆ Require processors to label poultry and meat: "Thoroughly cook this food to destroy harmful bacteria. Wash hands, dishes, and implements with soap and water immediately after contact with raw product."

◆ Set tight standards for microbiological contaminants in fresh and processed poultry and meat.

◆ Systematize safety standards for all foods. To assure an emphasis on public health rather than product promotion, the FDA (not USDA) should be charged with setting standards for and evaluating the operation of inspection programs for all foods, including fresh and processed meat, poultry, fish, and eggs.

◆ Require "traceback systems" that allow owners of contaminated animals to be identified, corrective action taken, and penalties enforced.

BRING BACK SAFE EGGS

It's a shame that eggs are so frequently contaminated with bacteria that they can no longer be safely enjoyed when raw or lightly cooked.

◆ Conduct the research and create the implementation programs necessary to eliminate bacterial contamination.

◆ Require that eggs be certified to be bacteria-free, or be labeled "Notice: Cook eggs thoroughly to kill bacteria. Do not eat raw eggs."

CREATE A STRONG FEDERAL
SEAFOOD-SAFETY PROGRAM

Fish is touted as the healthier alternative to meat, but much freshwater fish and some saltwater fish are contaminated with dangerous bacteria, industrial chemicals, or natural toxins. Eating raw shellfish is particularly dangerous.

◆ Establish an effective seafood-inspection program that focuses on preventing health hazards. New laws must protect whistleblowers and allow the public access to records.

◆ Extend and update standards for levels of microbes and chemicals.

◆ Reduce water pollution to reduce contamination.

◆ Tighten controls on imported and aquacultured seafood products.

◆ Warn raw-shellfish consumers of risks through warning labels on packages and signs at stores and raw-seafood bars.

DRUGS BELONG IN MEDICINE CHESTS, NOT IN FOODS

Many farm animals have a drug problem. And their problem becomes our problem if dairy products and meat are tainted. Drugs are sometimes used illegally, but even legal ones can endanger humans directly or by increasing the prevalence of bacteria that cannot be treated with common medications.

◆ Ban subtherapeutic uses in food animals of any antibiotics that might diminish the effectiveness of drugs for humans.

◆ Ban or establish lower tolerances for any drugs that pose significant risks to consumers.

◆ Phase out FDA's "extra-label drug use" policy, which a congressional committee called illegal.

◆ Enforce stiffer penalties for buyers and sellers of black-market veterinary drugs, which are illegal and may be dangerous.

◆ Improve and expand testing of milk and meat for illegal and dangerous veterinary-drug residues.

REDUCE PESTICIDE CONTAMINATION

Pesticides are inherently dangerous chemicals that inevitably contaminate our food. To obtain a safe food supply, the most dangerous pesticides should be banned and farmers should be encouraged to reduce or eliminate their use of all but the safest chemicals.

◆ Set a goal of slashing pesticide use in half by the year 2000, just as Scandinavian and other countries have done.

◆ Ban cancer-causing pesticides, unless reasonable substitutes (chemicals or other methods) are not available.

◆ Adequately test all existing and new pesticides for effects on the nervous system. Step up the re-evaluation of pesticides approved for use before adequate safety tests were required.

◆ Implement new national standards for organic-food production promptly.

◆ Tax pesticides and fertilizers; use the revenues to clean up the environment and to finance research on organic and sustainable agriculture and training programs for farmers.

◆ Require grocery stores to inform consumers of the presence on produce of post-harvest pesticides and waxes (which often lock in pesticides).

PROTECT CONSUMERS FROM DANGEROUS FOOD ADDITIVES

While most additives are safe, it doesn't make sense to add intentionally to our food supply chemicals that cause cancer or other serious or widespread health problems. Industry would like to weaken the law that bans cancer-causing additives.

◆ Save the "Delaney clause," which explicitly bans additives that cause cancer.

◆ Ban additives that pose unnecessary risks (and do not offer unique health benefits) or have not been adequately tested, such as certain food dyes, sodium nitrite, artificial sweeteners, BHA, BHT, and propyl gallate.

◆ Require that additives be licensed for a period of 20 years, rather than being approved permanently. Require that additives be tested in combination with aspirin, caffeine, BHT, and other chemicals that are widely consumed.

CONSIDER THE MOST VULNERABLE

Children are often at special risk since, among other reasons, they eat and drink more, relative to their size, than adults do, and since their bodies' defenses may not be fully developed. Farmers and farm workers encounter far larger quantities of pesticides than the rest of us do. Other groups of vulnerable people, including senior citizens and people infected with the AIDS virus, are increasing in numbers.

◆ Consider the most vulnerable members of society when setting limits on contaminants or additives in food.

◆ Put warning labels on those foods (raw shellfish and undercooked meat, poultry, and eggs) that pose the highest risks to vulnerable groups of people.

◆ Eliminate avoidable lead from the food supply. Children are highly susceptible to the toxic effects of lead. Food should not be packaged in lead-soldered cans or in plastic bags that are printed with lead-containing ink. Ceramics and crystal should be certified to not leach lead into food.

◆ The meager benefits of sulfites can't justify the risk of death to sensitive individuals. Ban remaining uses of sulfites that leave dangerous amounts in foods.

REQUIRE MORE AND BETTER FOOD LABELING

A Hostess Twinkie, cup of shortening, or bag of sugar may be totally free of bacteria, drugs, and pesticides, but it still isn't good for you. As we stated at the outset, the nutritional content of your diet has a greater impact on your overall health than most common contaminants do. Eat safely, but also nutritiously.

◆ Require more nutrition information: Meat and poultry labels, which are regulated by USDA, should provide the same nutrition information as the labels regulated by the FDA.

◆ Fast-food restaurants should provide complete nutrition information on their packages and on posters, as well as calorie listings on menu boards. Regular restaurants should provide nutrition and ingredient information for standard menu items.

◆ Alcoholic-beverage labels should list calorie contents and ingredients, along with notices warning consumers about links between alcohol and birth defects, cancer, hypertension, and other dangers.

DON'T LET INTERNATIONAL TRADE COME BEFORE INTERNATIONAL HEALTH

The safety of our food is reduced today by pesticides on imported foods and is threatened in the future by international-trade negotiations.

◆ Oppose "harmonization" of food-safety standards, which could ultimately pre-empt U.S. laws and reduce our standards to the "lowest common denominator" acceptable to foreign countries. The General Agreement on Tariffs and Trade (GATT) treaty, now being negotiated, has the potential to do this.

◆ Ban the sale to foreign nations of pesticides that are illegal for use in the United States, unless they won't end up in the imported food we eat and won't endanger the health of citizens in other nations. In any case, imported food should be more rigorously inspected.

AND ONE OTHER SPECIAL CONCERN...

◆ Tighten standards for bottled water, which should be at least as safe as tap water. Sodium and fluoride content and the source of water should be listed on all bottled-water labels.

HOW DO WE PAY FOR THESE REFORMS?

Ah, the perennial question! Here are just two ideas:

◆ Increase alcohol and cigarette excise taxes. This will do more than raise money—it will save lives. According to former Surgeon General C. Everett Koop, raising alcohol excise taxes is probably the single most effective way to reduce drinking-and-driving accidents.

◆ Increase federal fees for pesticide registration, and impose a new federal sales tax on pesticides and synthetic fertilizers.

Just by raising liquor tax rates to correct for inflation since 1970, and increasing wine and beer taxes to the liquor tax rate, we could raise an additional $22 billion annually and save more than $10 billion a year in costs attributable to alcohol problems. Taxes on pesticides and fertilizers could provide annual revenues of hundreds of millions of dollars to clean up the environment and assist farmers to switch to farming methods that use fewer potentially dangerous chemicals.

THE SAFE FOOD AGENDA BEGINS AT HOME

Accomplishing that action agenda would allow each and every American to rest much easier when he or she puts fork to mouth. But getting Congress and regulatory agencies to act is much easier said than done. The meat industry doesn't want any more inspectors breathing down its neck. The pesticide industry doesn't want to subject its products to more severe tests. Junk-food makers don't want to forgo additives that spell greater profits. Each of these industries employs skilled lobbyists who diligently argue their companies' cases to top officials.

The first message of *Safe Food* was to be a smart shopper, cook, and eater. The last message of *Safe Food* is to make your job as a consumer a lot easier by becoming a well-informed and active citizen.

CHAPTER 10
MORE FOOD
FOR THOUGHT
& ACTION

MORE FOOD FOR THOUGHT & ACTION

BOOKS AND REPORTS

Note: To order publications and other materials indicated below as available from CSPI, or to receive a complete listing of publications and materials available from us, please use the order form on the last page of this book. Make sure to indicate the quantity and price of each item requested.

NUTRITION

The Complete Eater's Digest and Nutrition Scoreboard, Michael F. Jacobson, Anchor Press, 1986. (Available for $11.95 from CSPI) *The Complete Eater's Digest* evaluates the safety of all common food additives; *Nutrition Scoreboard* gives at-a-glance ratings of the nutritional values of hundreds of foods.

Eater's Choice, Ron Goor, M.D., and Nancy Goor, Houghton Mifflin Co., 1987. Explains blood cholesterol levels and features recipes to lower and control cholesterol. Discusses the saturated-fat content of foods, outlines various risk factors of heart disease, and tells what to eat to follow the American Heart Association guidelines.

The Fast-Food Guide, Michael F. Jacobson and Sarah Fritschner, Workman Publishing, second edition, 1991. (Available from CSPI for $6.95) Complete nutritional analysis for virtually all foods offered by more than a dozen fast-food chains.

Jane Brody's Nutrition Book, Jane Brody, Bantam Books, 1987. (Available for $13.95 from CSPI) Comprehensive and accessible information on nutrition, including information on cholesterol, food additives, "health foods," vitamin supplements, and other issues. Some recipes included.

VEGETARIAN NUTRITION AND RECIPES

Fast Vegetarian Feasts, Martha Rose Shulman, Doubleday & Co., 1986. (Available for $12.95 from CSPI) Recipes for delicious, healthy, and inexpensive meals that can be prepared in less than an hour. (Includes fish and seafood recipes.)

The New Laurel's Kitchen, Laurel Robertson, Carol Flinders, and Brian Ruppenthal, Ten Speed Press, 1987. 500 recipes, plus informative text on diet and disease, diet during pregnancy, food for early childhood, and sports nutrition.

Simply Vegan, Debra Wasserman, The Vegetarian Resource

Group, 1991. (Available for $12 from The Vegetarian Resource Group, P.O. Box 1463, Baltimore, MD 21203) More than 160 recipes showing how to eliminate animal products and by-products from the diet. Contains a cruelty-free shopping-by-mail guide.

NUTRITION AND RECIPES FOR CHILDREN

Creative Food Experiences for Children, Mary Goodwin and Gerry Pollen, CSPI, 1980. (Available for $7.95 from CSPI) Activities, recipes, and games to foster good eating habits among children ages 3 to 10.

Eat, Think, and Be Healthy! Paula Zeller and Michael F. Jacobson, CSPI, 1987. (Available for $8.95 from CSPI) Dozens of activities and teachers' handouts that appeal to kids' imagination and sense of fun, while teaching the basics of good nutrition.

Kitchen Fun for Kids, Michael F. Jacobson and Laura Hill, Henry Holt & Co., 1991. (Available for $12.95 from CSPI) Recipes and nutrition facts to teach 7- to 12-year-olds good nutrition and self-sufficiency in the kitchen.

Organizing for Better School Food , CSPI's Children's Nutrition Project, CSPI, 1991. (Available for $7 from CSPI) A comprehensive plan of action for parents, activists, and food-service directors who are committed to improving school nutrition.

GENERAL COOKBOOKS

Deliciously Low, Harriet Roth, New American Library, 1983. Gourmet guide to low-sodium, low-fat, low-cholesterol, low-sugar cooking.

Healthwise Quantity Cookbook, Stephanie Turner and Vivian Aronowitz, CSPI, 1990. (Available for $29.95 from CSPI) More than 200 healthful recipes for feeding 50 people.

Jane Brody's Good Food Book, Jane Brody, Bantam Books, 1985. (Available for $14.95 from CSPI) 350 terrific recipes from *The New York Times'* personal-health columnist, showing how to cut down on fat, sugar, and salt; reduce the risk of diet-related illnesses; and achieve a normal body weight.

Jane Brody's Good Food Gourmet, Jane Brody, W.W. Norton & Co., 1990. (Available for $25 from CSPI) More than 500 recipes for healthful entertaining.

Louisiana Light, Roy F. Guste, Jr., W. W. Norton & Co. 1990. (Available for $25 from CSPI) 175 recipes for scrumptious Creole and Cajun food with no added fat, salt, or sugar.

Mediterranean Light, Martha Rose Shulman, Bantam Books, New York, 1989. Delicious recipes from around the Mediterranean basin that can make weight loss and good health painless and sensible.

The New American Diet, Sonja and William Connor, M.D., Simon & Schuster Inc., 1986. (Available for $12.95 from CSPI) 350 recipes showing how to reduce the risk of heart disease, lower blood cholesterol, lose weight, and protect against diet-related illnesses.

No Apologies Cookbook, Marcia Sabate Williams, The Crossing Press, 1986. (Available for $10.95 from CSPI.) 300 recipes to be enjoyed equally by people following Pritikin-type diets and those who don't want to bother checking fat or sodium.

20-Minute Menus, Marian Burros, Simon & Schuster, Inc., 1989. (Available for $19.95 from CSPI) 100 recipes by *The New York Times'* food writer and cookbook author for meals that are tasty, quick to prepare, and low in fat and sodium.

DIETARY SUPPLEMENTS

The Right Dose, Patricia Hausman, Rodale Press, 1987. Discusses using vitamins and minerals sensibly and safely. Includes buying guides and scores of recipes to reach recommended daily allowances naturally.

FOOD SAFETY

A Blueprint for Pesticide Policy: Changing the Way We Safeguard, Grow and Market Food, Public Voice for Food and Health Policy, 1989. Discusses pesticide-related health hazards and federal regulation, and proposes a comprehensive policy for change.

Circle of Poison, David Weir and Mark Schapiro, Institute for Food and Development Policy, 1981. Documents the international marketing of dangerous pesticides and citizen efforts to end the practice.

Eating Clean²: Overcoming Food Hazards, Center for Study of Responsive Law, 1987. (Available for $8 from the Center for Study of Responsive Law, Box 19367, Washington, DC 20036) An excellent 157-page compendium compiled by Ralph Nader and his colleagues, containing articles about food safety and nutrition.

For Our Kids' Sake, Anne Witte Garland and the Natural Resources Defense Council, Sierra Club Books, 1989. Step-by-step information on what to do—as a consumer and a citizen—about pesticides in children's food.

Keeping Food Fresh, Janet Bailey, Harper & Row, 1989. (Available for $10.95 from CSPI) How to select and store nearly every type of food.

On Food and Cooking, Harold McGee, Collier Books, 1984. (Available for $18.95 from CSPI) A comprehensive, yet entertaining, look into the science and lore of the kitchen.

Pesticide Alert: A Guide to Pesticides in Fruits and Vegetables, Lawrie Mott and Karen Snyder of the Natural Resources Defense Council, Sierra Club Books, 1987. Covers the most commonly used pesticides, including their health and environmental effects, how to reduce pesticide residues, and how pesticides are regulated.

Pesticide Perspectives: Pesticides in Food, Agroecology Program, University of California at Santa Cruz, 1990. (Free from the publisher, Santa Cruz, CA 95064) Addresses concerns about pesticide regulation, reduction of exposure to pesticide residue, interpretation of food labels and claims, and other issues.

The Wax Cover-Up: What Consumers Aren't Told About Coatings and Pesticides on Fresh Produce, CSPI, Americans for Safe Food, 1991. Gives background information and suggestions on how to get your supermarket to obey the wax-disclosure law.

WATER SAFETY

Drinking Water Hazards, John Cary Stewart, Envirographics, 1990. A comprehensive resource for determining if contaminants exist in drinking water, including information needed for making decisions about water testing.

Is Your Water Safe to Drink? Raymond Gabler, Ph.D., and the editors of Consumer Reports Books, Consumers Union, 1988. Examines the country's drinking-water problems. Includes information on bottled water, tests for determining drinking-water purity, and *Consumer Reports* ratings of water filters.

AGRICULTURE

Alternative Agriculture, National Research Council, National Academy Press, 1989. Reviews alternative farming methods used in the United States and concludes that such methods are practical and environmentally sound. Illustrates successes with 11 case studies and advocates wider adoption of alternative farming.

Animal Factories, Jim Mason and Peter Singer, Harmony Books, 1990. Exposes environmental, health, economic, and ethical costs of animal agribusiness. Outlines strategy for change for consumers and farmers.

Biotechnology's Bitter Harvest: Herbicide-Tolerant Crops and the Threat to Sustainable Agriculture, Biotechnology Working Group,

1990. (Available for $7 from Rebecca Goldburg, Environmental Defense Fund, 257 Park Ave. South, New York, NY 10010) Examines the extent of herbicide use, government and corporate research and development of herbicide-resistant plants, and the threats to health and the environment. Proposes alternatives to chemical weed control.

Diet for a New America, John Robbins, Stillpoint Publishing, 1987. Discusses the links between animal food production and the current epidemics of cancer, heart diseases, and other health problems. Criticizes inhumane treatment of livestock and the environmental impact of agribusiness.

Farms of Tomorrow: Community Supported Farms, Farm Supported Communities, Trauger M. Groh and Steven S. H. McFadden, Bio-Dynamic Farming and Gardening Association, Inc., 1990. Explores a new approach to farming, Community Supported Agriculture. Includes a list of resources for readers interested in initiating this approach.

ORGANIC GARDENING

Bug Busters, Bernice Lifton, Avery Publishing Group, Inc., 1991. Offers safe, natural, and effective solutions to bug and rodent problems in the house and garden.

The Child's Organic Garden, Lee Fryer and Leigh Bradford, Acropolis Books, 1991. A master gardener teaches his granddaughter and you how to raise nutritious, delicious, organically grown, pesticide-free vegetables.

The Cook's Garden, Shepherd and Ellen Ogden, Rodale Press, 1989. Gardening guide plus recipes to showcase the flavors of vegetables.

The New Organic Grower, Eliot Coleman. Chelsea Green, 1989. Tools and techniques for small-scale farming or serious home gardening. Covers crop rotation, green manures, market strategy, part-time help, and many other topics.

Rodale's Garden Problem Solver, Jeff Ball, Rodale Press, 1988. Quick and easy solutions, tips, and techniques for growing vegetables, fruits, and herbs.

Square Foot Gardening, Mel Bartholomew, Rodale Press, 1981. Shows how, based on a grid of one-foot squares, the square-foot garden produces as much food as a conventional row garden while requiring only one-fifth the space and work.

MAGAZINES AND NEWSLETTERS

Consumer Reports. $20.00/year. Consumers Union, 101 Truman Ave., Yonkers, NY 10703.

Nutrition Action Healthletter. $19.95/year. CSPI. Available from CSPI. See order form on the back page of this book.

Organic Gardening. $16.97/year. Rodale Press, 33 East Minor St., Emmaus, PA 18098.

Vegetarian Times. $24.95/year. P.O. Box 446, Mt. Morris, IL 61054-8081.

ORGANIZATIONS

CONSUMER ORGANIZATIONS WORKING ON FOOD SAFETY AND NUTRITION ISSUES

Center for Science in the Public Interest (CSPI) and **Americans for Safe Food,** 1875 Connecticut Ave., NW, Suite 300, Washington, DC 20009. (202) 332-9110. (For information on membership and publications, see the last page.)

Community Nutrition Institute, 2001 S St., NW, Suite 530, Washington, DC 20009. (202) 462-4700.

Consumers Union, 101 Truman Ave., Yonkers, NY 10703. (914) 378-2000.

Public Citizen, 215 Pennsylvania Ave., SE, Washington, DC 20003. (202) 833-3000.

Public Voice for Food and Health Policy, 1001 Connecticut Ave., NW, Suite 522, Washington, DC 20036. (202) 659-5930.

CONSUMER ORGANIZATIONS WORKING ON SPECIFIC FOOD-ADDITIVES ISSUES

Feingold Associates of the United States, P.O. Box 6550, Alexandria, VA 22306. (703) 768-FAUS or 1-800-321-FAUS.

National Organization Mobilized to Stop Glutamates (NOMSG), P.O. Box 1388, Santa Fe, NM 87504. 1-800-288-0718.

ORGANIZATIONS OPPOSING THE USE OF BGH/BST

Foundation on Economic Trends, 1130 17th St., NW, Suite 630, Washington, DC 20036. (202) 466-2823.

National Family Farm Coalition, 80 F. St., NW, Suite 714, Washington, DC 20001. (202) 737-2215.

National Farmers Union, 600 Maryland Ave., SW, Suite 202W, Washington, DC 20024. (202) 554-1600.

ORGANIZATIONS WORKING ON PESTICIDES, LEAD, AND OTHER CONTAMINANTS

Environmental Defense Fund, 257 Park Ave. South, New York, NY 10010. (212) 505-2100.

National Coalition Against the Misuse of Pesticides, 701 E St., SE, Suite 200, Washington, DC 20003. (202) 543-5450.

Natural Resources Defense Council, 40 West 20th St., New York, NY 10011. (212) 727-2700.

Rachel Carson Council, Inc., 8940 Jones Mill Road, Chevy Chase, MD 20815. (301) 652-1877.

U.S. Public Interest Research Group, 215 Pennsylvania Ave., SE, Washington, DC 20003. (202) 546-9707.

ORGANIZATION REPRESENTING GOVERNMENT AND INDUSTRY WHISTLEBLOWERS ON FOOD-SAFETY ISSUES

Government Accountability Project (GAP), 25 E St., NW, Suite 700, Washington, DC 20001. (202) 347-0460.

ORGANIZATIONS WORKING ON ALCOHOL ISSUES

CSPI's Alcohol Policies Project, 1875 Connecticut Ave., NW, Suite 300, Washington, DC 20009. (202) 332-9110.

The National Council on Alcoholism and Drug Dependence, 12 West 21st St., New York, NY 10010. (212) 206-6770.

ORGANIZATIONS WORKING ON VEGETARIANISM OR ANIMAL-WELFARE ISSUES

The American Society for the Prevention of Cruelty to Animals (ASPCA), 441 East 92nd St., New York, NY 10128. (212) 876-7700.

Food Animal Concerns Trust (FACT), P.O. Box 14599, Chicago, IL 60614. (312) 525-4952.

Friends of Animals (FOA), P.O. Box 1244, Norwalk, CT 06856. (203) 866-5223.

Humane Farming Association, 1550 California St., Suite 6, San Francisco, CA 94109. (415) 771-2253.

Humane Society of the United States, 2100 L St., NW, Washington, DC 20037. (202) 452-1100.

The Vegetarian Resource Group, P.O. Box 1463, Baltimore, MD 21203. (301) 366-VEGE.

ORGANIZATIONS WORKING ON SUSTAINABLE AGRICULTURE AND ALTERNATIVES TO PESTICIDES

Alternative Farming Systems Information Center, National Agricultural Library, Room 304, 10301 Baltimore Blvd., Beltsville, MD 20705, (301) 344-3704.

Appropriate Technology Transfer for Rural Areas (ATTRA), P.O. Box 3657 Fayetteville, AK 72702. (501) 346-7570 or 1-800-346-9140.

Bio-Integral Resource Center (BIRC), P.O. Box 7414, Berkeley, CA 94707, (415) 524-2567.

Institute for Alternative Agriculture, 9200 Edmonston Road, Suite 117, Greenbelt, MD 20770. (301) 441-8777.

The Land Stewardship Project, 14758 Ostlund Trail North, Marine on St. Croix, MN 55047. (612) 433-2770.

Leopold Center for Sustainable Agriculture, 126 Soil Tilth Building, Iowa State University, Ames, IA 50011-1010. (515) 294-3711.

Organic Food Production Association of North America (OFPANA), P.O. Box 1078, 23 Ames St., Greenfield, MA 01301. (413) 774-7511.

Rodale Institute, 222 Main St., Emmaus, PA 18098. (215) 967-5171.

GOVERNMENT AGENCIES

Bureau of Alcohol, Tobacco and Firearms, 1200 Pennsylvania Ave., NW, Washington, DC 20226. (202) 566-7777.

Environmental Protection Agency (EPA), 401 M St., SW, Washington, DC 20460. (202) 382-2090.

Federal Trade Commission (FTC), Pennsylvania Ave. and 6th St., NW, Washington, DC 20580. (202) 326-2222.

Food and Drug Administration (FDA), Department of Health and Human Services, 5600 Fishers Lane, Rockville, MD 20857. (301) 443-3170.

United States Department of Agriculture (USDA), 14th St. and Independence Ave., SW, Washington, DC 20250. (202) 447-2791.

HOTLINES

1-800-843-8114 or, in Washington, D.C., (202) 328-7744: American Institute for Cancer Research (AICR) Nutrition Hotline. Answers questions on personal nutrition and health.

Provides a variety of free publications, such as "Dietary Guidelines to Lower Cancer Risk," "All About Fat and Cancer Risk," and others. (AICR is a nonprofit, privately-funded, grant-making organization that sponsors research.)

1-800-4-CANCER: National Cancer Institute (NCI) Cancer Information Service (CIS) Hotline. Answers questions on cancer diagnosis, treatment, and diet. Provides a variety of free publications in English and Spanish, such as "Diet, Nutrition & Cancer Prevention: The Good News," "Everything Doesn't Cause Cancer," and "Cancer Facts for People Over 50." (NCI is part of the U.S. Department of Health and Human Services, National Institutes of Health.)

1-800-EAT-FISH. Provides a variety of free recipe booklets; not recommended for information on seafood contaminants. (Sponsored by the Seafood Council, an industry trade organization.)

1-800-622-DASH: Mrs. Dash Sodium Information Hotline. Answers general questions on low-sodium diets, and on the sodium content of more than 10,000 foods. A free brochure with recipes, diet hints, and coupons is available. (Sponsored by the Alberto Culver Co., the maker of Mrs. Dash salt-free herbs, spices, and sauces.)

1-800-858-PEST: National Pesticide Telecommunications Network (NPTN) Hotline. Answers questions on pesticides, toxicology, and environmental degradation. Provides several free publications, such as "Citizen's Guide to Pesticides." (Sponsored jointly by the U.S. Environmental Protection Agency and the Texas Tech University Health Sciences Center School of Medicine.)

1-800-288-0718: National Organization Mobilized to Stop Glutamate (NOMSG) Hotline. (Leave message.) Answers questions on MSG. A quarterly newsletter is available to members. (NOMSG is an educational and advocacy organization formed by MSG sufferers.)

1-800-535-4555 or, in Washington, D.C., (202) 447-3333: USDA's Meat and Poultry Hotline. Answers questions on safe handling of meat and poultry, such as cooking and storage temperatures, understanding labels, coping when the refrigerator fails, and others. Provides free publications, such as "A Quick Consumer Guide to Safe Food Handling," "Preventing Foodborne Illness," and others.

1-800-SAY-NO-TO: National Clearinghouse for Alcohol and Drug Information Hotline. Answers questions about alcohol and other drugs. Provides access to the Prevention Materials Database, maintains annotated bibliographies, distributes grant applications, offers information on local prevention and treatment resources. Provides more than 100 free publications. (The

Clearinghouse is the information component of the Office for Substance Abuse Prevention of the U.S. Department of Health and Human Services.)

1-800-426-4791 or, in Washington, D.C., (202) 382-5533: EPA Safe Drinking Water Hotline. Answers questions related to water quality and purity. Provides information on federal and state regulations, helps locate local certified labs for water testing. Provides free publications such as "Lead and Your Drinking Water," "Is Your Drinking Water Safe?" "Citizen Monitoring: Recommendations to Household Well Users," and others.

POSTERS AND SOFTWARE

"Anti-Cancer Eating Guide." (Available for $4.95 from CSPI) Poster tells which foods to eat and which to avoid to lower your risk of developing cancer.

"Chemical Cuisine." (Available for $4.95 from CSPI) Poster evaluates the safety of dozens of the most common food additives.

"Fast-Food Eating Guide." (Available for $4.95 from CSPI) Wall chart compares the nutrient values of more than 200 popular brand-name fast foods.

"Nutrition Scoreboard." (Available for $4.95 from CSPI) Chart rates the nutritional values of more than 200 foods.

"Michael Jacobson's Nutrition Wizard." (Available for $99.95 from CSPI) Software for IBM-PC compatible computers, for professional or home use. A nutrition analysis and diet planning system with a 1,800-food database.

"The DINE System for Macintosh." (Available for $219.95 to $269.95 from CSPI) Nutrition analysis program developed by researchers at the State University of New York at Buffalo.

MAIL-ORDER SUPPLIERS OF ORGANIC FOOD

The following growers and distributors ship their organic products directly to individual consumers, usually via UPS, and do not require a minimum order unless otherwise noted. Write or call them for complete product listings.

A note about organic certification: Until new national standards for producing organic food go into effect in 1993 (see page 53), certification of organic food will vary. Certification methods are indicated for each of the following suppliers. "C" indicates that all listed products have been certified organic by an independent certifying organization or agency. Suppliers that establish their own organic standards are considered self-certified, and are labeled with an "S." "V" indicates that certification varies and that products are labeled accordingly.

A listing in this directory does not constitute an endorsement by the authors, publishers, or the Center for Science in the Public Interest. We cannot guarantee the quality, purity, or supply of these companies' products.

ARIZONA

Arjoy Acres
HCR Box 1410
Payson, AZ 85541
(602) 474-1224
Garlic, dried beans and peas. (S)

ARKANSAS

Dharma Farma
Star Route Box 140
Osage, AR 72638
(501) 553-2550
Apples, pears. (C)

Eagle Agricultural Products
2223 N. College
Fayetteville, AR 72703
(501) 442-6792
Fresh and dried produce, beans, grains, pasta, flour. (V)

Good Earth Association
202 E. Church St.
Pocahontas, AR 72455
(501) 892-9545
(501) 892-8329
Corn, beans, seed crops. (S)

Mountain Ark Trading Company
120 South East Ave.
Fayetteville, AR 72701
AR: (501) 442-7191
US: 1-800-643-8909
Grains, beans, seeds, wide selection of products. (V)

CALIFORNIA

Ahler's Organic Date Garden
P.O. Box 726
Mecca, CA 92254-0726
(619) 396-2337
Dates, date products. (S)

Blue Heron Farm
P.O. Box 68
Rumsey, CA 95679
(916) 796-3799
Almonds, walnuts, oranges. (C)
Minimum order varies.

Covalda Date Co.
P.O. Box 908
Coachella, CA 92236
(619) 398-3441
Dates, dried fruits and nuts. (S)

Capay Fruits and Vegetables
23800 State Hwy. 16
Capay, CA 95607
(916) 796-4111
Dried tomatoes, peaches, herbs. (C)

Ecology Sound Farms
42126 Road 168
Orosi, CA 93647
(209) 528-3816
528-2276
Oranges, plums, Asian
pears, kiwi fruit, persimmons. (C)
Minimum order 8-40 lbs.
depending on item.

Frey Vineyards
14000 Tomki Road
Redwood Valley, CA
95470
(707) 485-5177
Wine. (C)
Minimum order ½ case

Gold Mine Natural Food
Co.
1947 30th Street
San Diego, CA 92102
1-800-475-FOOD
Brown rices, beans, macrobiotic items, wide variety of goods. (V)

Gravelly Ridge Farms
Star Route 16
Elk Creek, CA 95939
(916) 963-3216
Produce, grains. (C)

Great Date in the
Morning
P.O. Box 31
Coachella, CA 92236
(619) 398-6171
Dates. (C)

Green Knoll Farm
P.O. Box 434
Gridley, CA 95948
(916) 846-3431
Kiwifruit. (C)
Minimum order 7.5 lbs.

Jaffe Brothers
P.O. Box 636
Valley Center, CA 92082-0636
(619) 749-1133
Dried fruit, nuts, grains,
beans, assorted goods. (S)

Living Tree Centre
P.O. Box 10082
Berkeley, CA 94709
(415) 420-1440
Almonds, almond butter,
pistachios, apple trees. (C)

Lundberg Family Farm
P.O. Box 369
Richvale, CA 95974-0369
(916) 882-4551
Rice and rice products.
(C)

Mendocino Sea
Vegetable Co.
P.O. Box 372
Navarro, CA 95463
(707) 895-3741
Wildcrafted sea vegetables
(harvested seaweed). (S)

Natural Gardening
Company
217 San Anselmo Ave.
San Anselmo, CA 94960
(415) 456-5060
Vegetable seedlings. (C)
Minimum order 1 flat.

Old Mill Farm School of
Country Living
P.O. Box 463
Mendocino, CA 95460
(707) 937-0244
Lamb, goat cheese, produce. (C)
Minimum order $50.

Steven Pavich and Sons
Rt. 2, Box 291
Delano, CA 93215
(805) 725-1046
Grapes. (C)

Sleepy Hollow Farm
44001 Dunlap Road
Miramonte, CA 93641
(209) 336-2444
Apples, cooking herbs.
(C)
Minimum order 1 box.

Soghomonian Farms
8624 S. Chestnut
Fresno, CA 93725
(209) 834-2772
Grapes in season, raisins.
(C)

Timber Crest Farms
4791 Dry Creek Road
Healdsburg, CA 95448
(707) 433-8251
Wide variety of dried
fruits and nuts. (S)

Weiss' Kiwifruit
594 Paseo Companeros
Chico, CA 95928
(916) 343-2354
Kiwifruit. (C)
Minimum order 2½ lbs.

COLORADO

Malachite Small Farm
School
ASR Box 21, Pass Creek
Road
Gardner, CO 81040
(719) 746-2412
Honey, quinoa, beef. (S)

Wilton's Organic
Potatoes
Box 28
Aspen, CO 81612
(303) 925-3433
Potatoes. (C)
Minimum order 5 lbs.

CONNECTICUT

Butterbrooke Farm
78 Barry Road
Oxford, CT 06483
(203) 888-2000
Vegetable seeds. (C)

FLORIDA

Sprout Delights
13090 N.W. 7th Ave.
Miami, FL 33168-2702
(305) 687-5880
1-800-334-2253
Full line of bakery items.
(S)
Minimum order $20.

Starr Organic Produce
P.O. Box 561502
Miami, FL 33256-1502
(305) 262-1242
Wide variety of fruit. (S)
Minimum order 20 lbs.

HAWAII

Hawaiian Exotic
Fruit Co.
Box 1729
Pahoa, HI 96778
(808) 965-7154
Dried pineapples,
bananas, papaya, fresh
ginger root, turmeric. (S)
Minimum order 10 lbs.

IDAHO

Ronnigers Seed Potatoes
Star Route
Moyie Springs, ID 83845
(208) 267-7938
Vegetables. (S)
Minimum order $10.

ILLINOIS

Green Earth Natural
Foods
2545 Prairie Avenue
Evanston, IL 60201
1-800-322-3662
(708) 864-8949
Fresh produce, meats,
wide variety of items. (V)

Nu-World Amaranth
P.O. Box 2202
Naperville, IL 60540
(708) 369-6819
Amaranth flour, cereal,
whole grain. (C)

IOWA

Frontier Cooperative
Herbs
P.O. Box 299
Norway, IA 52318
1-800-365-4372
(319) 227-7991
Herbs, spices, teas. (V)

Nature's Korner
R2 Box 302
Iowa Falls, IA 50126
(515) 648-9568
Large selection of gro-
ceries, specializes in
breads. (S)

Paul's Grains
2475-B 340 St.
Laurel, IA 50141
(515) 476-3373
Whole grains and grain
products, beef, lamb,
chicken, turkey. (S)

KENTUCKY

Gracious Living Farm
General Delivery
Insko, KY 41443
Vegetables. (S)

Prosperity Farms
550 Gardener Road
Magnolia, KY 42757
(502) 528-2422
Condiments, pesto, pick-
les, salsa, etc. (S)
Minimum order varies.

MAINE

Crossroad Farms
Box 3230
Jonesport, ME 04649
(207) 497-2641
Root crops, squash, cab-
bage, apples. (C)
Minimum order $25.

Fiddler's Green Farm
R.R. 1, Box 656
Belfast, ME 04915
(207) 338-3568
Whole grain mixes, cof-
fee, syrup, and jam. (V)

Johnny's Selected Seeds
Foss Hill Road
Albion, ME 04910
(207) 437-4301
Vegetable, herb, and farm
seeds. (S)

Maine Coast Sea
Vegetables
Shore Road
Franklin, ME 04634
(207) 565-2907
Sea chips, kelp, dulse,
nori. (S)

Simply Pure Food
RFD #3, Box 99
Bangor, ME 04401
(207) 848-7371
Strained and diced baby
foods, baby cereals. (C)

Wood Prairie Farm
RFD 1 Box 164S
Bridgewater, ME 04735
(207) 429-9765
Maple syrup, oats and oat
products, various vegeta-
bles. (C)

MARYLAND

Macrobiotic Mall
18779-C N. Frederick
Ave.
Gaithersburg, MD 20879
(301) 963-9235
Grains, legumes, packaged
foods, macrobiotic items.
(C)

Organic Foods Express
11003 Emack Road
Beltsville, MD 20705
(301) 816-4944
Produce, grains, beans,
coffee, assorted goods. (V)

MASSACHUSETTS

Baldwin Hill Bakery
Baldwin Hill Road
Phillipston, MA 01331
(508) 249-4691
Sourdough bread. (C)
Minimum order 6 loaves.

Cooks' Maple Products
Bashan Hill Road
Worthington, MA 01098
(413) 238-5827
Maple syrup. (S)

Greek Gourmet, Ltd.
5 Pond Park Road
Hingham, MA 02043
(617) 749-1866
Extra virgin olive oil,
olives. (S)
Minimum order 1 case.

MICHIGAN

Country Life Natural
Foods
109th Ave.
Pullman, MI 49450
(616) 236-5011
Bulk natural foods. (V)

Eugene and Joan Saintz
2225 63rd
Fennville, MI 49408
(616) 561-2761
Fresh produce in season.
(S)

Todd Gulich
Nature's Market Whole
Foods
139 West Auburn
Rochester Hill, MI 48307
(313) 852-9327
Produce, meats, grains,
herbs, and other foods.
(V)

MINNESOTA

Diamond K Enterprises
R.R. 1 Box 30A
St. Charles, MN 55972
(507) 932-4308; 932-
5433
Grains and grain prod-
ucts, nuts, dried fruits.
(C)

French Meadow Bakery
2610 Lyndale Ave., So.
Minneapolis, MN 55408
(612) 870-4740
Many sourdough breads.
(C)
Minimum order $20.

Living Farms
Box 50
Tracy, MN 56175
US: 1-800-533-5320
MN: 1-800-622-5235
Grains, sprouting seeds.
(V)

Mill City Sourdough
Bakery
2070 Grand Ave.
St. Paul, MN 55105
(612) 699-4784
1-800-87-DOUGH
Sourdough breads. (C)
Minimum order 6 loaves.

Natural Way Mills, Inc.
Rt. 2, Box 37
Middle River, MN 56737
(218) 222-3677
Whole grains, flours, cere-
als, other products. (C)

MONTANA

The Good Food Store
920 Kensington
Missoula, MT 59801
(406) 728-5823
Beans, grains, dried fruits
and vegetables, cereals,
coffee and tea, pasta,
seeds, spices. (V)
Minimum order $25.

NEBRASKA

Do-R-Dye Organic Mill
Box 50, Route 1
Rosalie, NE 68055
(402) 863-2248
Oats, wheat, rye, corn
products. (S)
Minimum order $5.

M and M Distributing
RR 2, Box 61-A
Oshkosh, NE 69154
(308) 772-3664
Whole grain amaranth.
(S)
Minimum order 25 lbs.

Stapelman Meats
Rt. 2, Box 6A
Belden, NE 68717
(402) 985-2470
Beef, pork. (S)

NEW HAMPSHIRE

Water Wheel Sugar
House
Rt. 2
Jefferson, NH 03583
(603) 586-4479
Maple syrup. (S)

NEW JERSEY

Simply Delicious
243 A N. Hook Rd.,
Box 124
Pennsville, NJ 08070
(609) 678-4488
Wide variety of items. (V)

NEW MEXICO

Blue Corn Trading
Company
Box 951
Taos Pueblo, NM 87571
(505) 758-4803
Blue corn flour, herbs. (S)

NEW YORK

Bread Alone
Rt. 28
Boiceville, NY 12412
(914) 657-3328
Wheat, rye and sour-
dough breads. (C)
Minimum order 12
loaves.

Community Mill and
Bean
267 Rt. 89 S
Savannah, NY 13146
(315) 365-2664
Flour, mixes, beans,
grains, cereals. (C)
Minimum order $10.

Deer Valley Farm
R.D. 1
Guilford, NY 13780
(607) 764-8556
Meats, produce, grains,
baked goods, wide variety
of products. (V)
Minimum order $10.

Four Chimneys Farm
Winery
RD #1, Hall Road
Himrod, NY 14842
(607) 243-7502
Wine, grape juice, wine
vinegar. (C)
Minimum order for juice
1 case.

Gaeta Imports Inc.
141 John St.
Babylon, NY 11702-2903
(516) 661-2681
1-800-669-2681
Capers, porcini, olives,
and olive oil. (V)

**NORTH
CAROLINA**

American Forest Foods
Corp.
Rt. 5, Box 84E
Henderson, NC 27536
(919) 438-2674
Shiitake and oyster mush-
rooms, mixes, spices. (C)
Minimum order 10 packs.

OHIO

Earth's Best
Hand in Hand Catalogue
9180 LeSaint Dr.
Fairfield, OH 45014
1-800-543-4343
Baby food: purees, cereals,
juices. (C)
Minimum order 12 jars.

OREGON

Dement Creek Farms
Box 155
Broadbent, OR 97414
(503) 572-5564
Beans, grains, vegetables,
herbs. (C)

Herb Pharm
20260 Williams Hwy.
Williams, OR 97544
(503) 846-6262
Herbs, herbal extracts,
teas. (C)
Minimum order $25.

Mountain Springs
P.O. Box 861
Prineville, OR 97754
1-800-542-2303
Canned and smoked rain-
bow trout. (S)

River Bend Organic Farm
and Country Store
2363 Tucker Road
Hood River, OR 97031
(503) 386-8766
Fresh fruit, jams, syrup. (C)

PENNSYLVANIA

Dutch Country Gardens
Box 1122 Road #1
Tamaqua, PA 18252
(717) 668-0441
Potatoes, carrots. (S)
Minimum order $25.

Garden Spot Distributors
438 White Oak Road
New Holland, PA 17557
(717) 354-4936
Wide variety of dried and
packaged goods. (V)

Genesee Natural Foods
R.D. 2, Box 105
Genesee, PA 16923
(814) 228-3200
228-3205
Beans, grains, flours,
honey, pasta, cereals,
dried fruit. (V)
Minimum order $20.

Krystal Wharf Farms
RD 2, Box 2112
Mansfield, PA 16933
(717) 549-8194
Grains, beans, nuts, dried
fruit, seeds, fresh produce,
and other products.
(C)(S)

Rising Sun Distributors
P.O. Box 627
Milesburg, PA 16853
(814) 355-9850
Produce, dried fruit, nuts,
beans, grains, other items.
(V)

Walnut Acres
Walnut Acres Road
Penns Creek, PA 17862
(717) 837-0601
Full line of cereals, flours,
grains, baked goods,
soups, vegetables, other
items. (S)

PUERTO RICO

Finca del Seto Cafe
P.O. Box 30
Jayuya, PR 00664-0030
Whole and ground coffee.
(S)

TEXAS

Arrowhead Mills
Box 2059
Hereford, TX 79045
(806) 364-0730
A wide variety of grains
and grocery items. (C)

Stanley Jacobson
1505 Doherty
Mission, TX 78572
(512) 585-1712
Grapefruit and oranges.
(C)
Minimum order ¼ bushel.

Lee's Organic Foods
Box 111
Wellington, TX 79095
(806) 447-5445
Fruit jerkies. (C)
Minimum order $25.

VERMONT

Gourmet Produce Co.
RR 3, Box 348
Chester, VT 05143
(802) 875-3820
Sunflower and radish
sprouts, wheatgrass and
wheatgrass juice. (C)

Hill and Dale Farms
Rt. 2, Box 1260
West Hill–Daniel Davis
Road
Putney, VT 05346
(802) 387-3817
Apples, vinegar. (S)
Minimum order 1 flat
(24) apples.

Northeast Kingdom
Organic
RR1, Box 608
Hardwick, VT 05843
(802) 472-5710
472-6019
Root cellar vegetables,
dried beans and herbs,
canned goods. (C)

Teago Hill Farm
Barber Hill Road
Pomfret, VT 05067
(802) 457-3507
Maple syrup. (S)

VIRGINIA

Golden Acres Orchard
Rt. 2, Box 2450
Front Royal, VA 22630
(703) 636-9611
Apples in season, cider
vinegar, juice. (S)

Golden Angels Apiary
P.O. Box 2
Singers Glen, VA 22850
(703) 833-5104
Five types of honey. (S)

Natural Beef Farms
4399-A Henninger Court
Chantilly, VA 22021
(703) 631-0881
Frozen meats, produce,
bread, wide variety of
items. (C)

WASHINGTON

Cascadian Farm
P.O. Box 568
Concrete, WA 98237
(206) 853-8175
Fruit conserves, dill pick-
les. (C)

Homestead Organic
Produce
2002 Road 7 NW
Quincy, WA 98848
(509) 787-2248
Onions, garlic, apples. (C)
Minimum order varies.

Sunny Pine Farm
Rte. 2, Box 280
Twisp, WA 98856
(509) 997-1011
Garlic and garlic prod-
ucts. (C)

WEST VIRGINIA

Brier Run Farm
Rt. 1, Box 73
Birch River, WV 26610
(304) 649-2975
Goat cheeses (Chavre).
(C)
Minimum order $25.

Hardscrabble Enterprises,
Inc.
Route 6, Box 42
Cherry Grove, WV 26804
(304) 358-2921; (202)
332-0232
Dried shiitake mush-
rooms. (S)
Minimum order 1 box
(1½ lbs.).

WISCONSIN

Joel Afdahl
Route 1, Box 1580
Hammond, WI 54015
(715) 796-5395
Maple syrup. (S)

Nokomis Farm
3293 Main Street
East Troy, WI 53120
(414) 642-9665
Grains, breads, beef, pork.
(C)

SAMPLE LETTERS TO REGULATORS AND ELECTED OFFICIALS

You may want to write to the FDA, the USDA, and your Congressional representatives to ask them to do a better job of protecting our food supply. Such letters are most effective if you use your own words, but here are some sample letters to help inspire you. In addition, on page 223 we have included a sample letter to your supermarket manager.

TO YOUR SENATORS OR REPRESENTATIVE

Honorable _____
U.S. Senate
Washington, DC 20510
or
Honorable _____
House of Representatives
Washington, DC 20515

Dear Senator (or Representative) _____:

Numerous government reports have documented the inadequacies of America's food-safety system. As a result, thousands of people die from food-borne illnesses each year, and many more are likely harmed by pesticides and food additives that cause cancer, birth defects, and other problems. Frankly, I'm tired of the food scares that we're subjected to on an all-too-regular basis.

I urge you to support legislation that would reduce risks from bacteria and chemicals in our food. I also urge you not to support legislation that would make our food less safe, such as repeal of the Delaney amendment.

While adequate food-inspection programs and pesticide-residue standards are critically important, it is especially important to help farmers reduce their reliance on dangerous pesticides, veterinary drugs, and other chemicals. Not only do those chemicals endanger consumers, but they also endanger farmers and harm the environment. The federal government should help farmers to switch to organic or sustainable methods. One sensible strategy would be to tax pesticides and fertilizers. The resulting higher costs of those chemicals would help reduce their use, and the revenue raised could finance a large-scale movement to sustainable farming methods.

TO THE FDA

Commissioner David Kessler
Food and Drug Administration
5600 Fishers Lane
Rockville, Maryland 20857

Dear Commissioner Kessler:

The FDA plays a critical role in protecting the safety of America's food. Despite government claims that America has the world's safest food supply, each year thousands of Americans die unnecessarily from food-borne illnesses and chemical contaminants and additives. As someone who is literally fed up with scares about bugs, drugs, additives, and toxic chemicals in food, I urge you to make the FDA a crusader for food safety.

For starters, the FDA should inspect a larger fraction of fresh produce, especially imported produce, for pesticides. Moreover, the FDA must develop systems for preventing contaminated foods from reaching the marketplace. It's ridiculous to have a system that finds problems, but doesn't keep illegal foods out of our stomachs. The FDA should also ban dangerous veterinary drugs; crack down on the widespread illegal use of these drugs; and prohibit the routine feeding of antibiotics to poultry and livestock. I want the drugs I take to come from my doctor, not from drinking a glass of milk.

I also urge you to strengthen the FDA's program to ensure the safety of seafood. Because consuming raw shellfish poses such a high risk, the FDA should require packages and retail shops to display a sign warning of the danger, especially to people with AIDS or liver disease. The FDA should also do whatever it can to ensure that seafood is free of PCBs and other dangerous chemicals, as well as dangerous bacteria and viruses.

Hazardous or poorly tested food additives should be the easiest problems to deal with, but time and time again the FDA has bent over backwards to excuse the use of questionable additives. The FDA should ban uses of additives (such as BHA and sulfites) that pose a risk to some or all Americans. It should also require better testing of the artificial sweeteners aspartame and acesulfame K. Finally, I urge you not to seek to weaken the Delaney amendment, which bans cancer-causing additives. It simply doesn't make sense to add to our food chemicals that pose even the slightest risk of cancer.

TO THE USDA

Secretary Edward R. Madigan
U.S. Department of Agriculture
14th St. and Independence Ave., SW
Washington, DC 20250

Dear Secretary Madigan:

The USDA holds a critical position in America's food-safety system. However, considering the periodic food scares Americans have been subjected to in recent years, the USDA needs to do a much better job protecting our food.

I'm especially concerned about bacterial and pesticide contaminants. It's shameful that raw eggs pose fatal risks and that large percentages of chicken are contaminated with bacteria. The USDA must do a better job inspecting meat and poultry, and should insist that farmers and processors prevent contamination in the first place.

Until our food supply is largely free of germs, I urge the USDA to require a label notice on all fresh poultry and meat advising consumers to "wash hands and all cooking implements after contact with raw product."

And while you're thinking about food labels, please support legislation that would require nutrition labels on all fresh and processed meat and poultry products. The format should be identical to the one the FDA requires.

Pesticides leave unwanted residues on our food, and also endanger farmers and the environment. Please help farmers cut back on their use of pesticides (as well as animal drugs and chemical fertilizers). The USDA should mount vigorous programs to help farmers use sustainable or organic farming methods. For starters, the USDA should promptly implement steps that would establish a national definition of "organic" food, as required by the 1990 Farm Bill.

TO YOUR SUPERMARKET MANAGER

Dear Supermarket Manager:

    I shop at your store, but I am very concerned about problems of bacteria in poultry and meat, pesticide residues in produce, veterinary drugs in meat and milk, and unsafe additives in processed foods.

    I urge you to disclose the use of wax on produce (as required by federal law), and to place notices on all packages of eggs, poultry, meat, and raw shellfish advising consumers how to handle these foods safely.

    I ask you to do all you can to offer safer foods, organic foods, and foods free of questionable additives—especially in your store-brand products. Also, please relay my concerns to the president of your company. And please let me know of any progress along these lines.

NOTES & SOURCES

ABBREVIATIONS

CDC ....Centers for Disease Control
EPA ....Environmental Protection Agency
FDA ...............U.S. Food and Drug Administration
GAO ..............U.S. General Accounting Office
HHS ..............U.S. Department of Health and Human Services
HR .................U.S. House of Representatives Committee on Government Operations
JAMA ....*Journal of the American Medical Association*
NCI ....National Cancer Institute
NAS ....National Academy of Science
N Engl J Med..*New England Journal of Medicine*
NTIS..............National Technical Information Service
NYT ....*The New York Times*
OTA ....Congress of the U.S. Office of Technology Assessment
USDA ............U.S. Department of Agriculture
WSJ ....*The Wall Street Journal*

CHAPTER 1: SAFE FOOD CHOICES

1. *Food Technology* 41: 116, Nov 1987.
2. *Science* 250: 900, 1990.
3. *Science* 236: 289, 1987.
4. *Nutrition Action Healthletter:* 1, Jul/Aug 1990.
5. *Science* 251: 10, 1991.
6. 2, 3, 7, 8-tetrachlorodibenzo-p-dioxin (2, 3, 7, 8-TCDD) is the most toxic of the dioxins.
7. *Risk Analysis* 8: 485, 1988.
8. *Pesticide Residues in Food: Technology for Detection* (OTA): 9 and 223, Oct 1988.
9. Ibid., 13.
10. Ibid., 225.
11. *Clinical Microbiology Reviews* 1: 378, 1988.
12. *WSJ:* A1, Nov 16, 1990.
13. "Update: Salmonella Infections and Shell Eggs—United States, 1990," *Morbidity and Mortality Weekly Report* 39 (CDC): 1990.
14. *Seafood Safety* (GAO): 34, 1988.
15. *Alcohol* 7 (3): 277, 1990.

CHAPTER 2: FRUIT, VEGETABLES, & GRAINS

1. *Diet and Health: Implications for Reducing Chronic Disease Risk* (NAS): 8, 1989.
2. David Pimentel et al., "Environmental and Economic Impacts of Reducing U.S. Agricultural Pesticide Use," *CRC Handbook of Pest Management in Agriculture,* 2nd edition, vol. 1, David Pimentel, ed.: 679–718, 1991.
3. *Pesticide Industry Usage and Sales: 1988 Market Estimates* (EPA): 1989.
4. Pimentel et al, op. cit.
5. *Pesticides in Ground Water Data Base 1988 Interim Report* (EPA): 3, Dec 1988.
6. "First National Survey of Drinking Water Wells Shows Some Contamination by Pesticides and Nitrates," *EPA Environmental News,* press release: Nov 13, 1990.

7. *EPA's Groundwater Survey Tells Only Half the Story About Agricultural Chemicals*, press release (National Wildlife Federation, Natural Resources Defense Council, and Friends of the Earth): Nov 13, 1990.
8. Pimentel et al, op. cit.
9. *Pesticide Resistance*, (NAS): 12, 1986.
10. Pimentel et al, op. cit.
11. *List of Chemicals Evaluated for Carcinogenic Potential*, Memorandum from Reto Engler, Chief, Science Analysis Coordination Branch, Office of Pesticide Program [updated using the Integrated Risk Information System (IRIS), an EPA database]: March 9,1990.
12. *Regulating Pesticides in Food: The Delaney Paradox* (NAS): 1987.
13. "Report of the Cancer Risk Work Group," *Unfinished Business: A Comparative Assessment of Environmental Problems,* app. I (EPA): 1987.
14. *Epidemiology* 1: 349–56, 1990.
15. *JAMA* 256: 1141–7, 1986.
16. *Journal of the NCI* 82: 840–8, 1990.
17. *Science* 229: 257, 1985.
18. *Neurotoxicity* (OTA): 26, 1990.
19. Garth Youngberg, *Report and Recommendation on Organic Farming* (USDA): 1980.
20. *The Organic Farming and Produce Market* (Marketdata Enterprises, Inc., Valley Stream, NY): 35 and 39, Jan 1990.
21. Pimentel et al, op. cit.
22. *The Amicus Journal* 2: 40, Spring 1989.
23. M. J. Coye, *Journal of Public Health Policy* 6: 354, 1985.
24. "First Two Pesticides Eligible for Reregistration under FIFRA '88," *EPA Press Advisory:* Jan 25, 1991.
25. *Pesticides: Need to Enhance FDA's Ability to Protect the Public from Illegal Residues* (GAO): 1986.
26. Ibid., 3–4.
27. *Pesticides: Better Sampling and Enforcement Needed on Imported Food* (GAO): 3–4, 1986.
28. *Federal Register* 52 (77): 13305, 1987; and 54 (224): 48314, 1989.
29. *Intolerable Risk* (Natural Resources Defense Council): 1989.
30. *Consumer Reports* 54: 288, May 1989.
31. *Alternative Agriculture* (NAS): 12–13 and 19–20, 1989.
32. Robert Vanden Bosch et al., *Investigation of the Effects of Food Standards on Pesticide Use*, NTIS PB-278-976 (EPA): 114, 1978.
33. *Who Chooses Your Food* (California Public Interest Research Group): 24, 1978.
34. *Federal Food, Drug, and Cosmetic Act of 1938,* sec. 403 (i)(2) [See also 21 CFR 101.100 (a)(2), and *U.S. Food and Drug Administration Compliance Policy Guide* 7120.08: Oct 1, 1980].
35. *Cancer Research* 50: 6882–93, 1990.
36. *Consumer Reports* 55: 588, Sep 1990.
37. *Science* 251: 10, 1991.
38. Ibid., 606.
39. Ibid., 388.
40. *Science* 250: 744, 1990.
41. "Farmers' Markets: Good for Growers, Shoppers, and Cities," *NYT:* C9, Oct 3, 1990.
42. *Toxicants Occurring Naturally in Foods* (NAS): 1973.

CHAPTER 3: MILK & CHEESE

1. *Diet for a New America* (Stillpoint Publishing): 110, 1987.
2. BS stands for Bacillus stearothermophilus.
3. *FDA Surveys Not Adequate to Demonstrate Safety of Milk Supply* (GAO): 3, 1990.
4. "FDA Plans a Nationwide Test of Milk for Antibiotics, Other Drug Residues," *WSJ:* 10, Dec 28, 1990.
5. *FDA Regulation of Animal Drug Residues in Milk: Hearing Before the Human Resources and Intergovernmental Relations Subcommittee* (CGO): Feb 6, 1990.
6. *Human Food Safety and the Regulation of Animal Drugs Report,* 99th Congress, 1st session (HR): 99–461, 1985.
7. Ibid., Testimony of Michael F. Jacobson.
8. "Dairy Dilemma," *WSJ:* 1, Dec 29, 1989.
9. *FDA Surveys Not Adequate to Demonstrate Safety of Milk Supply:* op. cit., 3.
10. *Biotechnology and Milk: Benefit or Threat?* (Consumer Policy Institute, Consumers Union): 1990.
11. *Nutrition Action Healthletter:* 8, Apr 1991.
12. *Alternative Agriculture* (NAS): 169, 1989.
13. *JAMA* 258: 3274, 1987.

CHAPTER 4: MEAT, POULTRY, & EGGS

1. *Clinical Microbiology Reviews* 1 (4): 387–90, 1988.
2. "Biological Control Could Reduce Food Safety Problems of Poultry," *Science Report* (University of Wisconsin, Madison): Dec 10, 1990.
3. *Morbidity and Mortality Weekly Report* 38 (CDC): 878–880, 1990.
4. *Human Health Risks with the Subtherapeutic Use of Penicillin or Tetracyclines in Animal Feed* (NAS Institute of Medicine): 3, 1988.
5. Ibid., 59.
6. *Alternative Agriculture* (NAS): 168, 1989.
7. *Clinical Microbiology Reviews* 1 (4): 381, 1988.
8. *JAMA* 261: 1313–1320, 1989.
9. *Science* 249: 24, 1986.
10. *N Engl J Med* 311: 617–22, 1984.
11. *N Engl J Med* 316: 565–70, 1987.
12. "Drug-Resistant Salmonella in the US: An Epidemiologic Perspective," *Science* 234: 969, 1986.
13. *Human Health Risks with the Subtherapeutic Use of Penicillin or Tetracyclines in Animal Feed:* op. cit., 165.
14. "Test Case for a Crackdown on Drugs for Animals," *NYT:* 1, Apr 24, 1989.
15. *Human Food Safety and the Regulation of Animal Drugs Report,* 99th Congress, 1st session (HR): 99–461, 1985.
16. *Casarett & Doull's Toxicology: The Basic Science of Poisons,* 3rd edition, Macmillan Publishing Co.: 270, 1986.
17. Jim Mason and Peter Singer, *Animal Factories* (Harmony Books): 71, 1990.
18. "Pesticide Barred in '70s is Found to Taint Poultry," *NYT:* A16, Mar 16, 1989.
19. *Chemosphere* 17: 263, 1988.
20. *Human Food Safety and the Regulation of Animal Drugs Report:* op. cit.
21. *Imported Meat and Livestock: Chemical Residue Detection and the Issue of Labeling* (GAO): Sep 1987.

22. *Pesticide Residues in Food: Technology for Detection* (OTA): Oct 1988.
23. "Food Safety and Inspection Service (FSIS): Monitoring and Controlling Pesticide Residues in Domestic Meat and Poultry Products," USDA *Inspector General Audit Report:* Nov 1988.
24. *Alternative Agriculture,* op. cit.
25. *Poultry Inspection: The Basis for a Risk-Assessment Approach* (NAS press release): Mar 11, 1987.

CHAPTER 5: FISH & SHELLFISH

1. *Seafood Safety: Seriousness of Problems and Efforts to Protect Consumers* (GAO): 24, Aug 1988.
2. *Plan of Operations: NMFS Model Seafood Surveillance Project* (National Marine Fisheries Service): 1989; and *National Food Review* 11 (4): 33, 1988.
3. *Seafood Safety* (NAS): 6, 1991.
4. Ibid., 7.
5. *N Engl J Med* 319: 1228, 1988.
6. *Residues in Food* (FDA): 1989.
7. "The Truth About Seafood," *Garbage:* 27, Sep/Oct 1989.
8. *Environmental Toxicology and Chemistry* 8: 1, 1989.
9. *Safe Seafood: An Analysis of FDA Strategy* (FDA): 6, 1989.
10. *Seafood Safety* (NAS): 27, 1991.
11. *Safe Seafood* (FDA): op. cit., 17.
12. *Seafood Safety* (NAS): 79.
13. *Safe Seafood* (FDA): op. cit.
14. *American Journal of Clinical Nutrition* 51: 1, 1990.
15. *Developmental Psychology* 20: 523, 1984.
16. *Seafood Safety* (NAS): 255.
17. Ibid., 155.
18. *Risk Assessment for 2378-TCDD and 2378-TCDF Contaminated Receiving Waters from U.S. Chlorine-Bleaching Pulp and Paper Mills* (EPA, Office of Water Regulations and Standards): Aug 1990.
19. *Environmental Health Perspectives* 45: 171, 1982.
20. *American Journal of Public Health* 79: 322, 1989.
21. *Seafood Safety* (NAS): 267.
22. *Seafood Safety: Seriousness of Problems and Efforts to Protect Consumers* (GAO): 30.
23. *Seafood Safety* (NAS): 266.

CHAPTER 6: WHAT'S SAFE TO DRINK?

1. "Nitrate in Ground Water in the U.S.," R. F. Follet, ed., *Nitrogen Management and Ground Water Protection:* 40–41 and 67, 1989.
2. *Survey of Bottled Water Sold in Massachusetts* (Massachusetts Department of Public Health, Division of Food and Drugs): Dec 1987.
3. *Survey of Volatile Chemical Compounds in Bottled Water Products Distributed in New York State* (New York State Department of Health, Bureau of Public Water Supply Protection): Jan 1987.
4. *Consumer Reports* 52: 44, Jun 1987.
5. *Morbidity and Mortality Weekly Report* 39 (CDC): 173, March 23, 1990.

6. *Healthy People 2000: National Health Promotion and Disease Prevention Objectives* (Public Health Service): 64, 1990.
7. *JAMA* 264: 2406, 1990.
8. *Dietary Guidelines for Americans,* 3rd edition, (USDA): 26, 1990.
9. *Lancet* 337: 141, 1991.
10. Charles P. Mitchell and Michael F. Jacobson, *Tainted Booze: The Consumer's Guide to Urethane in Alcoholic Beverages:* 1988.
11. *Nutrition Action Healthletter:* 8, Nov 1988.
12. L. D. Eigen, *Alcohol Practices, Policies, and Potentials of American Colleges and Universities: An Office of Substance Abuse Prevention White Paper* (HHS), 1991.
13. *Circulation,* vol. 80, supp. II: 86, 1989.
14. *Nutrition Action Healthletter:* 8, Oct 1990.
15. "PCBs, PCDDs, and PCDFs in Breast Milk: Assessment of Health Risks," *Environmental Health Series* 29 (World Health Organization): 1988.

CHAPTER 7: THE TRUTH ABOUT ADDITIVES

1. *Science* 207: 1487, 1980.
2. *Pediatrics* 83: 27, 1989.
3. "Defined Diets and Childhood Hyperactivity," *National Institutes of Health Consensus Development Conference Summary* 4 (3): 1982.
4. *Developmental Pharmacology* 3: 74, 1981.
5. *Regulatory Toxicology and Pharmacology* 1: 355–78, 1981.
6. *Nutrition Action Healthletter:* 1, Nov 1985.
7. *Lancet* 2: 1453, 1988.

CHAPTER 8: THE SAFE FOOD KITCHEN

1. *Consumer Reports* 55: 378, Jun 1990.
2. *Consumer Reports* 56: 141, Mar 1991.
3. "Keeping Up With the Microwave Revolution," *FDA Consumer:* 17, Mar 1990.
4. *Food Additives Contaminants* 4: 385, 1987.
5. *Seminars in Dermatology* 9: 197–205, 1990.

INDEX

STAY INFORMED WITH CSPI'S
NUTRITION ACTION HEALTHLETTER

For the latest information on food safety and nutrition, join Center for Science in the Public Interest (CSPI) and receive the *Nutrition Action Healthletter.*

Nutrition Action is an award-winning, 16-page illustrated newsletter that is published 10 times a year. It provides tasty, nutritious recipes, debunks deceptive ads, and gives you the lowdown on contaminants in your food. *The New York Times* has called *Nutrition Action* "the best known of the newsletters...the information is accurate, well written, and up-to-the-minute." The *Healthletter* is "...my personal favorite," says author Jane Brody, a columnist for *The New York Times.*

Beyond giving you the information that will improve your health, CSPI serves as your lobbyist and watchdog in Washington. CSPI helped put "organically grown" on the map, discovered and prompted actions to curb illegal drugs in milk, obtained restrictions on unsafe additives, fought for warning labels on alcoholic beverages, and improved food labeling. CSPI is working to make the political reforms outlined in Chapter 9 a reality. We hope you'll work with us by joining the 250,000 other concerned citizens who are CSPI members.

USE THE ORDER FORM ON THE REVERSE SIDE.

CSPI ORDER FORM

✓ PLEASE SEND ME:

❑ CSPI's latest catalog of publications (no charge)

❑ 1-year membership in CSPI—
(includes subscription to
Nutrition Action Healthletter)
Special half-price offer _____ @ $ 9.95 = _____

❑ Chemical Cuisine poster
(paper) _____ @ $ 4.95 = _____

❑ Chemical Cuisine poster
(laminated) _____ @ $ 9.95 = _____

❑ The Complete Eater's Digest
and Nutrition Scoreboard _____ @ $11.95 = _____

❑ Plastic cutting board 11"×17" _____ @ $14.95 = _____

❑ More copies of *Safe Food* _____ @ $ 9.95 = _____

❑ Other items:

_____ _____ @ $ ____ = _____

_____ _____ @ $ ____ = _____

_____ _____ @ $ ____ = _____

Postage & handling _____ @ $ 1.25 = _____

Total enclosed _____

_____
NAME

_____
STREET   APT

_____
CITY   STATE   ZIP

Mail this form and a check for the total amount to:
Center for Science in the Public Interest
1875 Connecticut Ave., N.W., Suite 300
Washington, D.C. 20009